Many plans fail since we make complicated plans in a hurry and try to implement these impractical plans half-heartedly.

Missed calls are missed opportunities—we do not respond to all the calls which is unprofessional since we are indirectly insulting the caller.

We may have done MBA from a premiere institute but are we prepared to perform mind blowing actions which are more important?

A slight push by the leader to a competent team-member makes a Big Difference in order to accomplish Greater Challenges.

We should love people and use things but we love things and use people.

A book which is both educative and interesting and shall help many progress professionally and personally.

—C.K. Jaipuria

Chairman,

Jaipuria Group of Companies

REVIEWS

Vijay Walia too presents his version of the formula for becoming a sales honcho, a spiritually evolved person and a great team leader. Peppered with anecdotes, case studies and parables this slim volume will appeal to wannabe "good guy" business magnate.

The Tribune 26th September'10

•

Simple yet effective tips for your business and personal life with attractive illustrations. Particularly interesting is the author's take on replacing telemarketing with sending gifts to prospective customers.

The Week 24th October'10

•

If the learnings touch your heart and soul and develops in you a firm conviction about their implementation then kindly do implement them whole heartedly and the benefits accrued shall bring about a very positive change in your personal and professional life.

The Pioneer 21th October'10

•

The book AN IDIOT WHO SOLD A SHIP is an interesting one. The author has used stories/ fables and his own personal experiences to put his message across. The instances he has cited in the book about Bollywood stars, value of commitment, his own marketing strategies, dreams and aspirations, friendship, family, karma and making a lasting impression on others are well coordinated. The examples cited in the book reflect the author's in-depth knowledge about human psychology, interpersonal skills and farsightedness. This book will definitely inspire a lot of people especially the people in the marketing field.

Dr. P. Nayak, Professor & Director I.T.S- Institute of Management, Greater Noida.

•

As the front cover page says 'Nothing Theoretical About It' it, in fact, does not contain any theory of sales and marketing or business techniques but it definitely contains practical application of some theories and their outcomes. The thought and the idea communicated in this book will certainly help many in leading a purposeful life and a highly successful professional life. Therefore the book definitely is worth a quick-read...

Business & Management Chronicle, March 2011

AN IDIOT WHO SOLD A SHIP

•

A key to skillful application of simple skills
for business, personal and professional growth

•

Learning the art of practicing excellence to succeed
eventually from the perspective of a genius

VIJAY WALIA

UNICORN BOOKS

Publisher
UNICORN BOOKS
F-2/16, Ansari Road, Daryaganj, New Delhi-110002
☎ 23275434, 23262683, 23262783 • Fax: 011-23257790
E-mail: info@unicornbooks.in • *Website:* www.unicornbooks.in

Distributor
Pustak Mahal®
J-3/16, Daryaganj, New Delhi-110002
☎ 23276539, 23272783, 23272784 • Fax: 011-23260518
E-mail: info@pustakmahal.com • *Website:* www.pustakmahal.com

Sales Centres
- 10-B, Netaji Subhash Marg, Daryaganj, New Delhi-110002
  ☎ 23268292, 23268293, 23279900 • Fax: 011-23280567
  E-mail: salespmahal@airtelmail.in, rapidexdelhi@indiatimes.com
- 6686, Khari Baoli, Delhi-110006
  ☎ 23944314, 23911979
- **Bengaluru:** ☎ 080-22234025 • Telefax: 080-22240209
  E-mail: pustak@airtelmail.in • pustak@sancharnet.in
- **Mumbai:** ☎ 022-22010941, 022-22053387
  E-mail: rapidex@bom5.vsnl.net.in
- **Patna:** ☎ 0612-3294193 • Telefax: 0612-2302719
  E-mail: rapidexptn@rediffmail.com
- **Hyderabad:** Telefax: 040-24737290
  E-mail: pustakmahalhyd@yahoo.co.in

ISBN 978-81-7806-205-1

Edition: March, 2011

Printed at : Param Offsetters, Okhla, New Delhi-110020

CONTENTS

Preface

Dear Reader,

I am grateful to you for starting to read a book which is not written by an author of repute but a common person who has practiced excellence for the past many years.

He is highly successful in his personal and professional life and believes more in the application of knowledge than merely having knowledge. Hence successes are the end product of using one's skills and continue using the skills and knowledge with excellence and focused efforts till it becomes a habit and gets deeply imbibed in one's personality and is reflected in our day to day actions and thoughts.

It is my privilege to apprise you that this is my first attempt to write a book. I am a novice in the field of writing but am certainly bestowed, by the blessings of the Almighty, with the rare acquisition of a successful career in the field of sales and the ability to cope with the various stressful circumstances which one has to face in professional as well as personal life, by virtue of my inner peace attained through spiritualism.

The many practical skills acquired during a successful journey in the field of sales and spirituality are enumerated in the book which everyone will find helpful in leading a successful personal and professional life.

We have got to put the various skills one is born with or has acquired to rigorous use and pursue the set objectives with untiring highly focused efforts of excellence to be a winner and to lead a peaceful, purposeful and successful life.

The thoughts and the ideas communicated in the book will certainly help many in leading a purposeful personal life and a highly successful professional life without making the various mistakes knowingly or unknowingly which one is prone to make out of the excitement to be successful.

There is no short term method to be successful but one needs to go through the ordeal of facing the unfavourable circumstances boldly and emerge victorious and not succumb to the pressures and end up being a victim. One needs to handle success also with extreme care to be more successful in future.

Do go through the contents of the book and put into action those thoughts which you want to implement in your day to day life, provided you have mustered the conviction and are really convinced of rewarding results.

The author owes a debt of deep gratitude to his reverend Guru and others spiritual persons, all his family members, friends and colleagues and above all the circumstances itself which had to be faced in his professional and personal life in order to emerge victorious and end up gaining the experience to be successful in future.

The idiot is grateful to his present master Sh. C.K. Jaipuria, Chairman, Jaipuria group of companies where the idiot is working for the past eleven years. Under the dynamic leadership of Sh. Jaipuria the idiot got an exposure to various fields which has strengthened his own belief. A slight push by the master makes a big difference and the idiot is motivated to accomplish more challenges.

The idiot is grateful to his reverend Guru Maharshi Vaithathri, an exponent of S.K.Y. (simplified kundalini yoga) meditation, for initiating him towards the journey of spiritualism by awakening his kundalini power and bestowing the spiritual power of merging the self or fractional consciousness with the total consciousness and become one with GOD.

My salutations to the Almighty for bestowing His benevolent grace by invoking an urge to pen down a book reflecting the thoughts nurtured in the subconscious mind and reflected in this book which may help many and its success may motivate the idiot to write more books in future.

Everyone needs to start some day and the idiot has started today to forge ahead in his journey of practicing excellence in the field of writing and be successful in the long run. Happy reading and still better the actions performed after reading this book.

If you can kindly communicate the actions planned or the success achieved or wisdom attained if any, after reading this book the idiot shall be grateful and shall feel ever obliged and shall owe you a debt of gratitude for your encouragement pushing the idiot further to attain greater heights in a relatively unknown field.

Your critical comments howsoever blunt shall be appreciated and are requested.

Successfully yours,

An idiot
E-mail: waliavijaykumar@yahoo.com

Introduction

"An idiot who sold a ship"

Live as if you were to die tomorrow.

Learn as if you were to live forever.

Idiots are in the news these days and are being discussed today in various circles in view of the super success of the movie *3 Idiots* which has been released recently and has broken all box office records. Idiot is an antonym of genius who do out of the box thinking and try different approaches away from mundane activities. After reading this book you will conclude that the Idiot is a GENIUS.

An idiot was born in a small town in Punjab, studied in various schools since his father who was in the air force was transferred every three years. The idiot did his schooling from an English medium central school after studying in government schools up to the 10th class and thereafter pursued courses in pharmacy and graduated from the University of Delhi. The idiot was very fond of acting during school days and participated in various cultural activities in school and college. He also quenched his thirst and passion of acting by appearing in various stage dramas during school& college days. He has also acted in many television dramas and serials as a casual artist.

The idiot's parents were very spiritual and were the disciples of Swami Chinmayananda and Swami Dayananda and the idiot got a rare gift to attend various discourses of the Great Masters.

The idiot at a young age may not have understood the meanings in the right perspectives but was highly impressed by these great personalities.

The idiot did the masters course in S.K.Y. (Simplified Kundalini Yoga) meditation and also learnt Brahmgyanam from his revered Guru Maharshi Vaithathri—an exponent of Brahamgyanam and S.K.Y. meditation. His holy institute Temple Of Consciousness is located in Aliyar, Pollachi district, Tamil Nadu. The idiot had been visiting the institute for a week every year for the past innumerable years to meet and be blessed by his Great Master.

Circumstances brought the idiot into the field of sales which requires acting to some extent and the idiot grew in the sales and spiritual environment and learnt innumerable selling skills and also progressed spiritually. The idiot acquired many skills during the class room trainings of MNC and National companies. His selling skills were further sharpened during the seminars organized by the companies where professional speakers were invited to provide greater exposure to the company's managers.

The idiot started his career as a medical representative in a MNC pharmaceutical company which was a great achievement in the seventies. The basic requirement of the job was to make product presentations in front of highly educated medical fraternity which meant indirectly teaching doctors, through well rehearsed dialogues and in-depth knowledge, about the company's products. The companies used to provide in depth trainings for one month in Mumbai.

The doctor either buys or prescribes the product and the patient buys the medicine from the chemist thus increasing sales of the company's products. In selling one comes across various instances which are very educative to lead a more purposeful life in general and which sharpens one's selling skills in particular. Sales personnel are known to have wider exposures since they come across persons of various traits in day to day life.

In our day to day life also we sell ourselves to others i.e. we try to influence the thought process of others by putting across our thoughts and views to friends, relatives, acquaintances, peers, subordinates, superiors, customers, children and above all one's spouse. In life we need to convince others or get convinced, learn from others or make others learn.

We need to influence others in some situations or get influenced by others in some circumstances. Human beings are born with certain qualities and traits and during their stay on this planet acquire certain qualities through constant learning both in professional as well as personal lives and ultimately leave the planet, which everyone has to one day, leaving their mark in the hearts of their near and dear ones.

Only the well framed and garlanded photograph shall decorate the wall, maybe for a few days, months or maybe years depending upon the actions performed and the thoughts pursued during our stay on this planet.

Persons who have lead a purposeful life without attachments to the materialistic world and made voluntary contributions to make this world a better place to live are said to have attained moksha i.e. they are free from this cycle of life and death which is the essence of teachings of all the religions.

Ik din bik jayega Maati ke mole
Jag me reh jayenge Pyare tere bol

One day you will be sold at the price of mud which fetches nothing in return.

What will remain in this world is just your voice which may echo in the hearts of those that loved you.

The human body has to perish one day and what shall remain in world are our noble thoughts if any.

Inborn and acquired practical skills are being reproduced in this book for the benefit of human beings in general and for those in sales in particular to achieve success through excellence.

The idiot started his career by selling medicines and has recently sold ship load of coal. He shall end up selling, may be ships at a later stage or a ship full of selling skills through this book and quite a few to follow. The idiot found that the field of sales is a very interesting field where there are innumerable opportunities of learning from real life situations which influence our thought processes and in turn we not only become good human beings but become highly competent in our interactions whether professional or personal.

The idiot was born in a religious family which practiced good virtues. The family had the privilege to be bestowed by the kind blessings of the Almighty. The idiot's parents were disciples of Great Saint Swami Chinmayananda who had enlightened the people all over the globe with his rare spiritual wisdom. Swami Chinmayananda was an exponent of the Philosophy of Bhagwad Gita and had conducted innumerable discourses propagating the teachings of the Holy Book.

We may have been born poor but must die rich. The money we earn and the reputation we build up by the continuous use of various skills inborn or acquired and put to actions to the best of our abilities during our stay on this planet is what matters. We should be remembered for the good actions we have performed diligently for the benefit of the society in general and our near and dear ones in particular.

We may be born ignorant but during our stay on the planet earth we have to attain enlightenment through spirituality. This can be done by performing good deeds and become one with the Almighty by getting rid of vices i.e. *Kaam*, *Krodha*, *Lobh*, *Moh* and *Ahankaar* which are the impediments in our journey of spirituality. All the religions preach good virtues and advocate various methods to be one with the Almighty by performing good deeds. Only the methodology may be different but the objective remains the same which is self realization.

All human beings are Karam Yogis i.e. persons performing actions or still better persons performing Mind Blowing Actions i.e. MBAs in the terminology of a Karam Yogi.

Chapter One

Plan Patiently and Implement Impatiently

Just having knowledge is not enough; what is of paramount importance is its application.

Planning hosh se karo aur implement josh se karo

Knowledge has also got to be applied with conviction and perseverance.

We may have done MBA from a premiere institute in India or abroad but in order to succeed we need to have the killer instinct i.e. to put the knowledge to rigorous practice.

In order to appease our parents in particular and the society in general we undergo the strenuous process of acquiring theoretical knowledge and become content by its mere acquisition. But thereafter we don't put the knowledge gained into practice in order to get tangible results thus failing to utilize the competency which ultimately dies within.

Facts are known to many but the fact remains we fail to act on them. The persons who act in spite of not knowing the facts are much better than the persons who do not act in spite of knowing the facts.

Be a person of action and act immediately. A person of action who tries in spite of not achieving success is far better than the all knowing person who does not act at all. In the process of trying we end up at least gaining experience decreasing our chances of failing in the future.

A candidate for the post of news broadcaster was rejected because of his voice. He was also told that with his obnoxiously long name, he would never be famous. *He was Amitabh Bachchan.*

A small boy, fifth among the seven siblings of a poor father, was selling newspapers in a small village to earn his living. He was not exceptionally smart at school but was fascinated by religion and rockets. The first rocket he built crashed. A missile he built crashed several times and he was often ridiculed. Undeterred he kept trying. He is the person to have scripted the space odyssey of India single handedly. *He was Dr. APJ Abdul Kalam.*

In 1944, Emmeline Snively, director of the Blue Book Modeling Agency told a modeling hopeful Norman Jean Baker "You should better learn secretarial work or get married". *She went on to become Marilyn Monroe.*

A school teacher scolded a boy for not paying attention to his mathematics and for not being able to solve simple problems. She told him that he would not achieve anything worthwhile in life. His mother, however, believed in him and coached him in mathematics. *He went on to become Albert Einstein.*

A four year old girl, 20th of the 22 children, contracted double pneumonia and scarlet fever which paralyzed her left leg. At the age of nine, she removed her leg braces and started walking somehow. At 13, she decided to become a runner but kept failing miserably in all the races she participated. She kept trying and finally started winning every race she entered. *She is Wilma Rudolf who went on to win three Olympic Gold Medals.*

In 1954, Jimmy Denny, manager of The Grand Ole Opry, fired a singer after only one performance. He told him "You ain't going nowhere ...son, you ought to go back to driving a truck". *He went on to become Elvis Presley.*

In 1962, four young musicians played their first record audition for the executives of Decca Recording Company. The executives were not impressed. While turning down this group of musicians one executive said "we do not like their sound. Groups of guitars are on the way out". *The group was called the Beatles.*

Had the above personalities quitted after initial failures, they would not have been what they are today? The secret of their success is that they did not quit and went on trying in spite of failures initially and emerged victorious finally.

Excellence in actions is the crux of any success. In case we fail to act how can we ever be successful? So in order to be successful act immediately.

We may all know the theories of swimming but to really swim we have got to jump in the water without which all the theories are futile.

We may know the molecular formula of water which is H_2O. We may know that water has two molecules of hydrogen and one of oxygen; but when we need to quench our thirst, mere knowledge of the formula of water will not serve any purpose. Our thirst can be quenched only when we drink water.

We initiate many things in our day to day life and make innumerable resolutions and excitedly follow the regime rigorously for only a few days but thereafter we don't have the patience to pursue our objectives further which is essential part of any resolution. This happens since the project or the resolution was started only out of excitement and not with a firm conviction or faith in the task undertaken.

These resolutions are nothing short of issuing a cheque of a bank where in we do not have an account—hence worthless.

We should start one thing at a time after our heart and soul is convinced about its benefits which have been viewed from all angles. All the pros and cons have to be evaluated before making any firm decision then and then only can we muster the conviction to implement it.

Today we plan in a hurry and the plans are so intricate and theoretical that though they may sound fantastic theoretically, they're not practical or worthy of implementation. What we fail to view of such plans is the practical aspects i.e. **implementation**? Since the plans are not practical and so complicated that our own as well as the team's commitment for implementation is at the lowest ebb and with a half-hearted approach in implementation, even the best of plans cannot deliver the results.

When a complicated and theoretical plan is implemented half-heartedly by any team it results in the bare minimum or virtually no results. On the other hand, a simple practical plan which is implemented with great gusto by a highly motivated team will result in accomplishing the desired results which in turn shall boost the morale of the team to implement any other plan.

One should not hesitate even to do the smallest jobs meticulously and excel in its implementation. When one does small jobs with excellence big things happen sooner or later. Implementation once initiated has to continue with dedication with all out efforts, clarity of vision and above all faith in oneself. Things are bound to happen if one goes all out to make things happen.

Today's corporate philosophy of: **Make things happen or things will happen to you**, can be conquered with patient planning and impatient implementation.

When one plan fails we immediately make another hurried theoretical plan and get this more complicated plan implemented through a more demoralized team which has failed in its first attempt and the second plan also fails and results in fiasco. This vicious cycle continues till a visionary or set of visionaries in the organization make a practical plan with great patience and make all the team members participate in the process of planning, inviting suggestions from the people who work at the grass root level.

The suggestions of the front line field force offer a value addition to the plan since suggestions from grass root level personnel are likely to be more practical as they interact with the customers directly. Ultimately a practical plan is chalked out and internally the team also gets highly motivated since they had been kept in the loop while making the plan. The team members are convinced since they start nurturing the feeling that it is **their own plan** which they implement wholeheartedly and with all the more enthusiasm and dedication.

Practical plans when implemented with great gusto deliver results which are par excellence which become a matter of astonishment for the other people in the organization as well as outside the organization viz. the competitors. The team wins kudos from everyone i.e. superiors, peers and subordinates and the team is fully charged to accomplish yet another challenge.

Thus practical planning and wholehearted implementation makes every plan a great grand success and the cycle continues. The individuals as well as the organization grow in revenues and profits and there is no looking back since the top lines and the bottom lines are taken care of which is the crux of any business i.e. to make profits and to continue making profits.

Once the idiot went with a friend to watch a movie shoot which was happening in a remote village in Punjab. The hero of the film was known to the idiot's friend. After reaching the location the friend introduced the idiot to the hero and they started chatting. Virender, the hero of the film was a relative of our favourite Dharamendra. The idiot also met Mr. Raza Murad, known in the film industry for his powerful dialogue delivery.

The idiot was surprised that Mr. Raza Murad had written all his dialogues in Urdu to be delivered in Punjabi since the shoot was that of a Punjabi movie. The idiot out of curiosity asked the hero as to what the story of the film was? The hero Mr. Virender said, to the amusement of the idiot, that he can bet Rs 100/- that even the director of the film can't narrate the story?

How can you shoot a film without a story wondered the idiot? It is a right case of enthusiastic implementation without any plan. Don't remember the box office success of the movie but certainly must have been a failure. How can any venture succeed without a plan?

Long term plans have to be fractionalized and have to be bifurcated into short term objectives and the results have to be reviewed periodically to monitor the progress.

Passion and Perseverance Pays

The idiot knows of a medical representative who in the good old days when the companies were not used to having customers data banks, had maintained a record of his customers wherein he had maintained the customer's profile with the customer's photographs. What passion and job involvement? Needless to add this medical representative was a star representative of the company and always excelled in achieving the objectives.

The idiot has been regularly sending birthday greetings for the last 38 years to his once Divisional Manager in Merck India an MNC and today Director of the company. Even after leaving MERCK 18 years ago the trend continues and during his visit to Mumbai where the Director resides the idiot makes it a point to visit him and his family, so strong is the relationship built out of trust, love, affection and without any ulterior motive but out of love and respect for one another.

Whether we are selling medicine, toothbrushes, combs, shaving razors, soft drinks, packaged drinking water, pet bottles or even coal, the basic skills required are the same.

The idiots sold all the above to his heart's content and baffled the people who matter in the organization as well as the marketplace.

If the legendary Amitabh Bachchan at the age of 67 years gets up at 5.30 a.m., goes to the gym and crams his lines in the corner of the film set after coming to the set on the dot, why can't others emulate this?

If SRK can develop six packs for his highly acclaimed movie *Om Shanti Om* why can't he be emulated by others?

If Aamir Khan can develop six packs for his highly successful film Ghajni. If the same hero can bring about the look of a young college student by shedding pounds of flab out of dedication and passion why cannot any one emulate?

If Prime Minister Manmohan Singh with an ordinary background can rise to the position of Prime Minister with conviction, dedication, perseverance, knowledge and above all its application in the desired direction why can't we?

Success is not accidental but the result of innumerable planned and implemented efforts.

Chapter Two

Know Your Team

Believing everybody is dangerous

Believing nobody is very dangerous

– Abraham Lincoln

Are your team members MBAs? The idiot is not asking whether our team members are Master of Business Administration degree holders? But here the terminology is a bit different:

M - Mind

B - Boggling

A - Actions

Are your team members ready to perform Mind Boggling Actions?

A successful team member needs to perform mind blowing actions in the marketplace which is virtually a battlefield for the guys in sales. These mind-blowing actions must be performed in the highly competitive and dynamic market amidst cutthroat competition and yield mindboggling results. The team leader must therefore prepare the team members to perform mind blowing actions in their assigned territories by becoming a coach, a facilitator and a motivator.

Know the Individuals in the Team

We can read Linda Goodman's *Sun Signs* to know the personality traits of our team members and get an idea as to **what makes them tick.** It's not necessary that we must read the book but we should be able to analyze others' personalities in order to understand their viewpoint or look at things and the situations from their perspective.

Although the leader should know the team members as individuals but team members have to work as a cohesive team and not as individuals. The team should work towards the achievement of one objective and all the energies of the team members have to be channelized in one direction i.e. in accomplishing the objective.

In some organisations the team members work as individuals and the team or the organization lacks team spirit and hence are not able to achieve objectives. Team members are busy driving their own individual agenda; therefore the team or organization's agenda takes a back seat and is never accomplished. Such teams or organizations end up becoming a losing team or organization and in the long run may perish altogether.

The above is not only applicable to the team but in personal and professional relationships as well. Many of the traits mentioned in *Sun Signs* are common in the various zodiac signs. The idiot strongly believes that it is good to know the birthdays and zodiac signs of our near and dear ones and then deal with them accordingly, be it your spouse, children, friends, relatives, peers, subordinates or even superiors.

Arians are known to possess very large egos and they are usually found to be highly domineering. They need to be tackled accordingly. Never ever hurt the big ego of an Arian and do not try to dominate them. Respect their ego and they shall act as you may desire. This may not be true of all Arians nevertheless, is a common trait in many.

Taureans are known for their patience which they have in abundance. Never ever take advantage to their patience because they may charge back with the rage of a bull and leave you permanently bruised. They are practical persons and may take time to arrive at a decision but once they decide then no one how so ever powerful can change them.

Scorpions are known for their passion, openness and politeness but they carry a firm stick. Never ever try taking a scorpion for a ride since once offended they have the rare virtue of stinging and shall leave you permanently injured. If they do not like a person they will try to avoid the person. They are highly passionate about people and are known to bestow their blessings on the talented persons and believe in building lifelong relationships. Scorpions are dynamic leaders and know how to get the best out of the teams or individuals. Their business acumen is par excellence

The idiot had the opportunity of working with two great Scorpions who could see the spark in the idiot and provided great support to him in spite of opposition and under unfavourable circumstances. It will not be out of context to mention the names of these great Scorpions to which the idiot owes a debt of deep gratitude. Mr. C. K. Jaipuria, the chairman of Jaipuria group of companies where the idiot is working for the last more than eleven years. And Mr. Vijay Kumar, Director Merck India Limited, an MNC and Germany based pharmaceutical company in which the idiot served for more than eighteen years.

Incidentally, Mrs Indira Gandhi, Shri Lal Bahadur Shastri & Pundit Jawaharlal Nehru were all scorpions and are even remembered today as truly great and charismatic leaders.

His present employer Shri C. K. Jaipuria has allowed the idiot to serve in his flagship company for eleven years and reposed his confidence in the idiot's abilities which the idiot reciprocated by putting in his best efforts with dedication and devotion and produced excellent results. With the kind blessings of his master the idiot could give impressive presentations in

India, Dubai and Germany which were applauded by one and all.

Sagittarians are known for their magnanimity and compassion. The idiot has two friends who are Sagittarians and they share a long term healthy relationship which has survived for more than forty years and the bond has only strengthened with the passage of time. One friend is in Delhi practicing medicine and is leading a purposeful life propagating SKY (Simplified Kundalini Yoga) meditation and the second is the owner of a well established factory in Bangalore.

A CEO of a company once on a round saw one of his employees simply sitting in the chair doing nothing. He asked the employee his salary and pat came the reply, 'Sir, Rs 20,000/- per month'. Notice period in the company was two months. Immediately the CEO took Rs 40,000/- from the cashier and gave it to the employee and told him that from the next day he need not come to the office since his services were not required any more.

Another employee who was watching the entire drama asked the CEO what he had done? The CEO replied he had simply sacked an employee who was found doing nothing.

"But Sir, he was not our employee but had come to deliver pizza and was waiting for his payment."

Although it is a joke but It carries a message that we should be able to distinguish between **our own employees** and outsiders. If it is already happening in your organisation, it is wonderful. The employees must be feeling good about it. Preferably the employees should be addressed by their first names. Nothing sounds better to the ears than our own sweet name.

The team leader should know all the team members as individuals i.e. at any given time he should be able to provide **SWOT** (Strengths, Weaknesses, Opportunities and Threats) analysis based upon the personality of that team member.

Appropriate tasks should then be allocated to the team members as per their talent, passion, skills.

For example: the computer savvy member should be given the task to prepare the data relating to sales. A team member who is good in making presentations should be given the task of making and presenting effective presentations before the team members. Similarly, the team members who are a good in communication and does quality oriented work should be given the task of handling the key accounts.

Once, the right responsibility is allocated to the right team member they will endeavour to excel in their activities, since the task has not been enforced upon them but has been delegated intelligently by the team leader as per their competency. Thus they will accomplish the task with **passion.** Persons who do their work with passion excel in accomplishing the task as they enjoy doing the assigned task to the bottom of their heart and soul.

The Perfect Boss

There were about 70 scientists working on a very hectic project. All of them were really frustrated due to the pressure of work and the demands of their boss but everyone were loyal to him and did not think of quitting the job.

One day, one scientist came to his boss and told him— Sir, I have promised my children that I will take them to the exhibition going on in our township. So I want to leave the office at 5:30 pm. His boss replied, "Okay, You're permitted to leave the office early today".

The Scientist started working. He continued his work after lunch. As usual he got involved to such an extent that he only looked at his watch when he felt he was close to completion. The time was 8.30 PM. Suddenly, he remembered the promise he had given to his children.

He looked for his boss, he was not there. Having told him in the morning itself, he closed everything and left for home. Deep within himself, he was feeling guilty for having disappointed his children. He reached home. The children were not there.

His wife was sitting alone in the hall and reading magazines. The situation was explosive; any talk would boomerang on him. His wife asked him, "Would you like to have coffee or shall I straightaway serve dinner if you are hungry.

The man replied "If you would like to have coffee, I too will have but what about Children?" The wife replied, "You don't know? Your manager came here at 5.15 pm and has taken the children to the exhibition"

What had really happened was, the boss who granted him permission was observing him working seriously at 5.00 PM. He thought to himself, this person will not leave his work, but if he has promised his children they should enjoy the visit to exhibition.

So he took the lead in taking them to exhibition. The boss does not have to do it every time. But once it is done, loyalty is established.

That is why all the scientists at Thumba continued to work under their boss even though the stress was tremendous.

By the way, can you hazard a guess as to who the boss was? He was none other than Dr. APJ Abdul Kalam, the former President of India who was also the mastermind behind India's successful weapons and missiles program?

Earn the Respect of the Team

A leader should set an example and should preach what he follows. Else he cannot earn respect from his team

This was a very popular drama among soldiers some time ago.

A Colonel is reprimanding the jawans in his room where he was sitting behind a table. To the first jawan he points out that his uniform is not ironed properly and orders him to get the uniform ironed and come to him. The second jawan whose shoes are not polished is ordered to get the shoes polished and report. Similarly the third jawan is told that the brass buttons of his uniform are dirty and sent to get them polished. The fourth jawan is reprimanded for his nails which are full of dirt and had not been cut for the past many days.

The colonel after having shouted at all the jawans for one reason or the other finally gets up to go for lunch. The audience used to be enthralled to see the colonel although fully dressed had forgotten to put on his trousers and was sitting behind the table only in underwear.

Moral: One must first ensure that the leader is following what he is preaching.

It has been seen that team leaders reprimand the team members for reporting late to the workplace whereas they themselves are always late. Also a team leader reprimands his team members for their rude behaviour whereas the leader himself may be very rude.

Who will have any respect for these kinds of team leaders? Who will pay heed to the teachings of such team leaders? They may have got the position of a team leader in the organization due to some reason or other but the **respect** needs to be earned by the behaviour, knowledge and other qualities possessed by the team leader.

The team leaders who are respected by their team members are highly successful in leading their teams to accomplish challenging tasks by becoming facilitators and motivators. Never ever ask one's team members to perform activities which one is not competent enough to demonstrate in practice.

If one is asking one's team member to get a particular revenue from a territory and the member is reluctant or is doubtful of this achievement then the leader needs to demonstrate the way to achieve better results and still better in case he can accompany the team member to the marketplace and show the team member by giving demonstrations in the market. What a great impact this will have on the entire team in general and the doubtful team member in particular?

A team leader who does not respect the feelings of his team members has no right to expect the respect from his team members.

Leader's Speed Determines the Team's Speed

When we meet people who are enthusiastic and cheerful we also become enthusiastic in their company where as in the company of persons who are negative we tend to become negative. In a bus in case we start yawning we will observe the person sitting next to us will also start yawning and may ultimately sleep.

Persons who get the opportunity to work under dynamic and passionate leaders end up emerging winners since they in turn start emulating the positive traits of their leader who is task as well team oriented.

Any weak link in the team can jeopardize the success of the whole team. This weak link needs to be made strong by counselling, demos, class room and workplace trainings and in case the weak link does not perform satisfactorily then he has to be replaced or may be assigned some other role in the team for the overall success of the team.

Identify the weak link in the team immediately and start the corrective action **yesterday** i.e. on topmost priority.

Two salesmen who were working for a shoe manufacturing company were sent to an island in order to explore the possibility and the potential of the shoe business. Both the salesmen were astonished to see that all the inhabitants of the island were walking barefooted and there did not exist a culture of wearing shoes at all.

Immediately the first salesman sent a SOS to his boss conveying that since no one wears shoes here, therefore there is no potential of selling shoes on the island and immediately returned to his headquarters.

The Boss was perplexed to receive a communication from the second salesman informing that the scope for shoes was unbelievable there since no one wears shoes and asking for a consignment of 1000 pairs of shoes to be immediately shipped to the island. Right enough a second consignment of shoes was also asked for by the salesman in a couple of days.

There are persons who see opportunity in adversity and the others who see adversity even in opportunity. Try to build up a team of members having the former traits.

Chapter Three

The Rare Power of Focus

To do two things at once is to do neither.

- Publilius Syrus

First and foremost we got to market our strategic planning to our team members as if it is **their own planning** so that the planning is implemented enthusiastically by the highly motivated team which creates a win-win situation for the organization as well as the team. The team members should be convinced to the core of their hearts that the plan is perfect and practical and shall yield the desired results.

In this case the soft drinks industry is the best example where the salesmen, executives and the managers get a feedback of the success of a plan on day to day basis. Targets are set on daily basis in the morning when the salesmen leave for the market and they report their achievements towards the end of the day. At times incentives are given on daily basis.

The performers are motivated by way of getting incentives in the evening and the non performers are counselled to achieve better results the next day by the concerned managers and executives.

Money won is twice as sweet as the money earned.

In other industries, where the targets are on a monthly basis, these should be further broken down into daily objectives and the progress should be reviewed on a daily basis so that the next day's plan and objective can be set accordingly.

One must set objectives every day and review the achievement daily in order to plan better for the next day. Priorities need to be made on a daily basis. One cannot do everything in a day therefore the need to prioritize.

It is better to write down the tasks to be performed as per the priority and towards the end of the day tasks accomplished should be struck off and the remainders should be carried forward to the next day agenda as per the priority. Time frames too can be allocated i.e. at what time will an objective be achieved? This is termed time management in modern management jargon.

In the soft drinks industry the managers and executives enquire about the sales figures achieved at any given time during the day from the salesmen. The salesmen can be contacted over mobile phones and in case of any doubt of the achievement of the pre-set objective during the day they rush and catch up with the salesman in the market. They help the salesman to achieve the day's objective and in turn earn the respect of the salesman. The executive and manager who do their jobs diligently by extending timely support to team members end up building winning teams.

The winning teams always work with a predefined focus which is deeply imbibed in the team member's hearts and souls—of course by the team leaders.

The sun's rays when focused through a magnifying glass have the power of setting on fire the piece of paper kept underneath these focused rays. Why then, can't the focused efforts of a highly charged team accomplish their goals in a manner that burns the competition? Such is the tremendous power of **focused efforts**.

The focused efforts of a highly focused team results in highly fruitful **results** in any organization, caring two hoots for the competitor's activities. These focused teams continue forging ahead in spite of the fierce efforts of the competition to distract their energies; since all the energy of the winning team is channelized in one direction i.e. in the pursuit of achievement of their goal and they keep moving undeterred and end up achieving their goal.

'The power of focus'

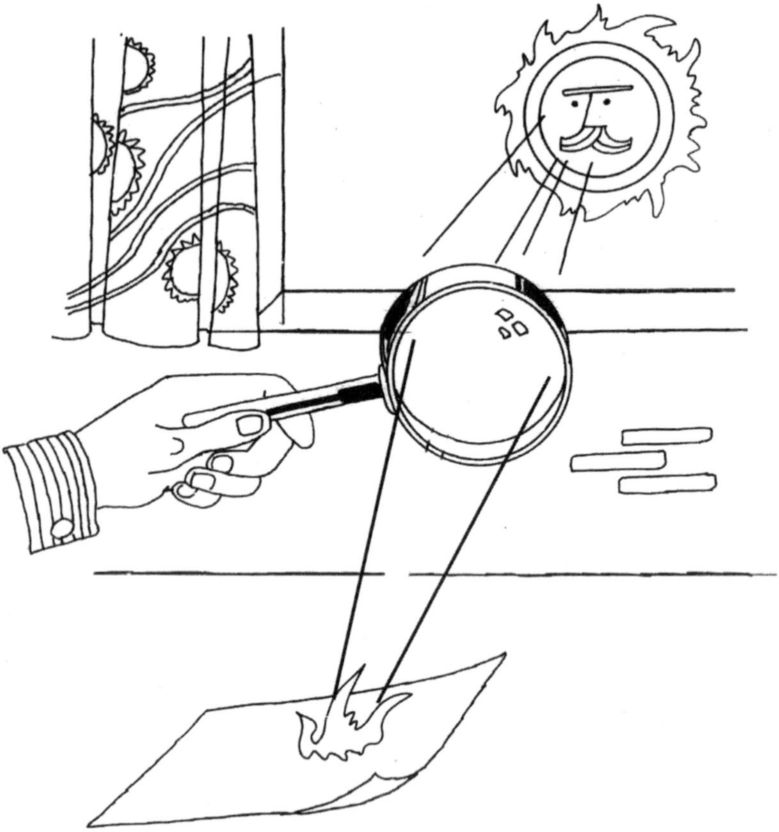

Focused persons, teams and the organizations attain success by putting in untiring efforts towards excellence.

Focus provides us the rare virtue of doing what we have decided to do and not to bow down to perceptions of what the others are thinking? Since all the energies have been channelized in one direction, negative feelings, back biting and organizational politics which is common in individuals, teams and organizations take a back seat and a positive environment prevails leading to success.

If we set multiple objectives then the energy possessed gets diluted and we may end up being unsuccessful and the individuals, teams and organizations may get demoralized in the long run.

Chapter Four

The Great Value of Commitments

Never break four things in your life—trust, promise, relation and heart because when they break they don't make noise but pains a lot.

– Charles

Ek baar mein commitment karta hoon to apne dil per likh deta hoon. —Once I commit I write it in my heart.

Please Do Not Back Out

We should always honour our commitments. How true is it for any one in personal or professional life i.e. always honour our commitments? Once we commit we should never ever back out. It is better not to commit than to back out at a later stage. In selling and marketing in case we have committed to a customer and honoured our commitment the customer develops trust in us and the relationship is strengthened. In case we do not stick to our words the customers loses faith in us and we need to make tiring efforts to bring the customer back which is sheer waste of energy.

The same is true in personal relationships as well. It takes years to build up relations and just a second to break them. We therefore must believe in making and not breaking relations.

There are other advantages of knowing the birthdays of our acquaintances in not only understanding them better but one is able to send birthday greetings so that the bond strengthens further and the relationship develops. It is true for the customers as well. Try sending a birthday greeting card to a customer and the result will be only positive. By sending greetings on various occasions we are indirectly telling the recipients the importance they have in our personal lives and as well as for our business association which a mutually shared benefit.

Small Gestures Make a Big Difference

Once the idiot had sent a birthday greeting card to one of his team members and was astonished at the results. The team member had tears in his eyes since it was the first birthday greeting card he had ever received in his life.

The idiot used to celebrate the success of the team by offering vegetable patties and pastries to the team members. It was a small gesture but the team members got so used to it that they made it a habit to complete the targets and once in a while if they could not they used to feel deprived of the petty celebration and used to avoid the idiot due to their unsuccessful attempt. In this scenario the idiot used to meet each and every team member in order to appreciate the efforts they had put in to accomplish the task and the team used to feel motivated to take up the next challenge.

Once one of idiot's team members met with a scooter accident and was admitted in a trauma centre. The idiot made it a point to visit the team member on three occasions and the family members of the team member still recall the small gesture with great pride. Needless to add the team member developed greater respect for his leader.

Once a very senior team member in peak summer developed symptoms of exhaustion and was so depressed and demoralized that he confided in the idiot that he is unable to cope up with the peak summer in the soft drinks company when the sales pressures are tremendous. Since he was not able to perform he started thinking of resigning. In summers it is very difficult for the field force to perform in a soft drink company due to extreme heat of April and May and greater sales pressures.

The idiot empathized with him and took him to his family physician at his own cost and sanctioned him three days' leave and the team member after taking the prescribed medicine reported for work in the pink of health and started working with renewed energy and of course became a personal friend too.

A peon's daughter died suddenly and the peon informed the idiot of the tragedy. The peon was very dear to the idiot. At the time of the daughter's death the idiot was travelling but he made it a point that someone attends the funeral and next day after his return visited the peon's family with his wife and spent couple of hours with the peon's bereaved family and offered their condolences and expressed their sympathies.

Missed Calls Are Missed Opportunities

Customers like employees are highly fragile and need to be handled with utmost care. Respect their feelings and never ever avoid any customer's telephone call. There are instances of customers getting annoyed when the salespersons do not take their call. It is an insult to the person whose call has not been taken. Today due to ego hassles and casual approach, there are many who never respond to the telephone calls by not picking up their cells. One must go through the number of missed calls on one's mobile phone to realise the number of customers and friends we have offended on that particular day.

We must therefore make it a point to at least respond to all the calls immediately by sending a message immediately communicating the reason for not taking the call. Thereafter we must respond to the call at our convenience by calling back the person, whether a customer, supplier, peer, subordinate, boss or friend. In case we do not want a person to call us then we should have the guts to tell that the person to not call again and provide the person the reason for not taking his calling.

Higher the numbers of unattended calls lower the productivity of the salesperson.

Chapter Five

Seize Each and Every Opportunity to Serve the Customer

The customer is obliging us by giving us an opportunity to serve him. Earn your customer's satisfaction.

We need to pay respect to our customers in one way or the other and always have to be grateful for the opportunity he has gracefully provided to us. One should always look for any opportunity to provide extra service to the customer and have an edge over our competitor.

Why should a customer buy your product when the same quality is available with the competitor at the same price?

In the above scenario it is the service which makes the difference. It is the transparency in business dealings which makes the difference. It is your careful and mature handling of the customer which is a fragile commodity, which makes the difference. It is the importance you give to the customer which makes the difference. It is the trust that the customer has developed in you which makes the difference.

Try assigning a highly productive territory to an average team and you will find in time to come the territory will end up becoming a low productive territory. Now allocate the same territory to a winning team and in time to come they shall make it the most productive territory in the organization.

Customer oriented strategies when implemented in the marketplace result in increased productivity. There is a great need to keep the customers satisfied. Satisfied customers are a great asset for the success of any business.

Satisfied customers have to be kept satisfied by the efforts of sales personnel. It is often seen that sales personnel in order to sell the product make tall claims and do not tell the facts to the customer and at a later stage the customer feels cheated. The sales personnel make commitments in the marketplace which they are unable to meet in the long run and the customers start distrusting them and in turn since the commitments are not honoured the customer develops distrust in the organization itself and may not buy the company's product at all.

Keep the customer satisfied as far as possible by providing a quality product at a reasonable price and above all par excellence service. There needs to be a win-win situation between the buyer and the seller so that the buyer gets a quality product at a reasonable price and the seller too makes some profit out of the sales; and this in turn shall lead to long term business relations and an increasing base of loyal customers.

How can you sell an inferior quality product to a customer at an inflated rate? It is a win-lose situation. How can you even sell a quality product to a customer at an inflated price? It is yet another win-lose situation. How can you even sell a quality product to a customer at a lower price wherein you do not make any profit and the customer has been passed on your profit in order to make a sale? It is a lose-win situation. How can you sell a quality product to a customer at a reasonable rate without the service which the customer looks forward to? It is a win-lose situation.

In all the above situations there is no win-win situation for the buyer and the seller hence there will exist only short term business relations and results will be only short term business dealing.

In the win-win situation the customer gets a quality product at a reasonable price and the supplier makes reasonable profit and also provides excellent after sales service if required.

24X7 Service—Sacrifice Time for Customers

During his tenure one of the reason why the idiot was successful in his mission in selling the pet preforms par excellence is the idiot worked 24X7 and not even a single call irrespective of the time was attended to by the idiot and responded by a concrete action plan.

The idiot got a call from a customer at midnight during the season and the customer wanted to know whether the vehicle containing pet preforms had left the company's works in Jammu that day. Instead of getting angry the idiot immediately contacted his works in Jammu and obtained the status from the works about the dispatch and confirmed the same to the customer at 12.25 am.

If a customer is frantically calling at midnight that means there must be genuine problem at his end and that needed to be responded at the earliest. Who attends to customer's phone calls at midnight? Only **idiots** since they tend to be different in order to build long term business relations.

In the above case the organization would not have any objection to idiot's not attending customer's call at midnight. The customer too would not have minded if his call was not taken at midnight. But the point to be pondered upon is the idiot never wanted to miss an opportunity to serve the customer by the professional services and in turn build long term business relations with the customer.

In case a customer gives an opportunity one must utilize it since it is the customer who has obliged us by giving an opportunity to serve him and not the other way around.

Personal Service—An Opportunity

There was a renowned doctor in a small town in Punjab who was the physician in the government hospital and had a roaring practice. The doctor had a relative in Delhi who needed one of the idiot's costly products. The doctor asked the idiot for

50 samples of the product i.e. Encephabol tablets. The idiot gave the samples to the doctor who in turn sent it to his relative living in Delhi. The idiot sensed the opportunity to serve his customer and asked the doctor's his relative's address in Delhi where the idiot would go once in two months to attend the company's conference.

There after the idiot started sending the samples to the relative directly through post parcel or at times delivered the samples personally going to the relative's house and giving Encephabol tablets samples which he did regularly for two to three years. The doctor was extremely pleased with the services and used to prescribe the idiot's company's products left, right and centre. The idiot too was extremely happy that he has won the customer.

Since the doctor was very competent he was promoted as the chief medical officer of Amritsar. In the meanwhile the idiot was also promoted and had to cover the city of Amritsar where the purchase budgets were huge. This doctor returned the idiot's personal service of sending Encephabol to his relative by giving an order for Rs Three lakhs at one go. One good turn deserves another.

What Makes The Customer Tick?

There was a doctor in Hoshiarpur, a small town in Punjab Dr Mrs X who actually was a midwife but had been carrying out delivery in her small hospital cum nursing home which was located in the fields with green surroundings. The idiot came to know that this doctor used to purchase medicines worth approximately Rs 7000/- in a month. The idiot decided to sell to this doctor and called upon the doctor on a couple of occasions but did not get any order. During the deliberation the idiot noticed the Doctor's inclination towards Congress in general and the charismatic Congress leader Mrs Indira Gandhi in particular.

Hencefort the idiot decided to talk less about his company's products and more about Mrs Gandhi and this strategy paid wonders. The doctor confessed to her admiration for Mrs Gandhi and the idiot walked away with an order of Rs 3000/- from the doctor which eventually the idiot was able to stretch to Rs 5000/-

In case we can understand what makes the customer tick you can be successful in winning the customer. In case we try to win the argument we may definitely win the argument but at the cost of losing the customer.

Never Offend the Customer

Moral: Never ever call a blind customer blind since the customer may get offended. It is always better to use the euphemisim 'Surdas' which is a refined form of blind.

Win the Customer and Lose the Argument

Salespeople at times act as know-alls which is not correct. It is better to lose the argument even if what we are saying is right and what the customer is saying is wrong. We, in order to prove the customer wrong, indulge in arguments and sometimes even succeed in winning them. Do we even stop to consider that we had gone to the customer to make a sale and not create a war-like situation by arguing? In case we agree diplomatically to the customer who may be wrong we will win the customer and will end up making a sale, succeeding in the achievement of our objective.

Chapter Six

Task Vs Team

In a day when you do not come across any problems, you can be sure that you are travelling on a wrong path

– *Swami Vivekananda*

Autocrats—the Intimidators

Every manager or leader has their own style of functioning. There are managers who are highly task oriented and are often termed as autocrats and are known to intimidate their team members to perform without showing them a way how to perform?

In this kind of leadership, the task is of prime importance and the team members are demanded to complete the task by hook or crook. Team members lead by autocrats usually function under extreme pressure and are bound to get mentally and physically tired.

They may complete the task under the whip of the team leader but will usually be insecure in this kind of atmosphere and will do mechanical jobs without any passion to work, since the leader is insensitive to the people and cares two hoots for his team members. The teams developed under such leadership may be efficient but not effective i.e. they may be doing the things rightly, but necessarily not the right things.

These so called leaders may succeed in their endeavours initially but are liable to be unsuccessful in the long run as

I shall kill you, if you don't lay two eggs each tomorrow

All the other hens have laid two eggs as per my instruction Why have you laid only one egg? I need an immediate answer or I shall kill you

Team members working under Autocrats or Intimidators feel very insecure due to fear and work pressure they may be one of the contributory factors for high employee turnover rate in their respective organizations.

Democrats—People Oriented

People oriented leaders are sensitive to the feelings of their team members but at times they become hypersensitive and may neglect the task itself. They are termed Democrats. These kind of teams may do the job effectively i.e. doing the right things but may not be efficient.

Leaders—Effective and Efficient

The ideal manager/team leader should have a balance of both: the task as well as the team. He should be able to get the assigned task accomplished while at the same time be sensitive to his team members feelings as well. Here the team members work both effectively as well as efficiently. When the right thing is done the right way by a passionate team the results are bound to be par excellence.

We cannot use the same stick for all the team members. A team leader needs to use different sticks to push different people. We should know the team members as individuals and handle the individuals accordingly. *Saam*, *Daam*, *Dand*, and *Bhed* the result have to be delivered whatever be the methodology.

A father and his 7 year old daughter were to cross a narrow wooden bridge built over a fast flowing river. The father told his daughter that she should hold his hand so that they could cross the river safely. The little daughter replied that instead of her holding his she would be more secure if he held her hand.

The father was a little confused and asked what the difference between the two was. There is a great difference said the daughter. "In case I hold your hand I may get frightened midway and may let go of your hand; but when you hold my hand, even in the worst of difficulties you will not let go of it and we can cross the river safely." Such was the daughter's faith in her father.

The team leaders should emulate this example and earn this rare virtue that all their team members should trust them in the event of any adversity whether personal or professional.

The team members should have unshakable faith in their team leader that in case of any eventuality the leader will not ditch them and will live up to the expectations of the team. If the team is successful a true leader gives all the credit to his team whereas in case of the team's failure he takes the blame on himself. This kind of team leaders are respected by each and every team player and always end up winners.

The same holds true for the elders in families. The members of the family should always have faith in the elders and the elders in turn should **give** and **take** instead of **take** and **give**. In other words, the elders should give more and take less from the younger ones of the family.

Chapter Seven

Satisfied Employees Are God's Gifts

Employee—a Highly Fragile Commodity

An employee in any organization is a rare commodity which needs to be handled very carefully since they are highly fragile. The more comfortable an employee is in the organization the more fortunate is the organization by way of excellent market image and sound bottom line and top line. These organizations are the ones making profits and shall continue making profits—the crux of any business.

Comfortable employees are dedicated to work for the realization of the vision and mission of any organization. We should keep our teams and employees comfortable and in turn they shall keep us comfortable by generating increased productivity.

In some companies there exists a culture of *chacha-bhateeja vad* where the favourite yet incompetent employees flourish under the shelter of their big uncles blocking the growth of many talented employees who are disheartened year after year and when are unable to bear the injustice either start speaking ill of the organization or quit the company itself, both of which are detrimental for the growth of any organization.

With this kind of culture we stimulate the secretion of adrenaline in the employees and the employee either resort to

fight or **flight** which is not a good sign for the prosperity of any organization.

The rage which a dissatisfied employee exhibits can shake, if not the heavens, then at least the organization itself.

These are the main reasons for unions making a back door entry. Satisfied employees are either God gifted or are groomed to become satisfied by the untiring efforts of the HRD. HRD should put in all out efforts to develop a team of satisfied employees with various initiatives.

HRD—Human Resource Development or Human Resource Deterrent

There was a company which had a good system of declaring the annual increments through the departmental heads. Each employee used to be called personally by the departmental head who communicated the increment awarded to the employee.

During one such increment announcement the departmental head called an employee and the employee was informed by the boss that in addition to a good increment, in view of the good work done by the employee, he had earned a promotion as well. The employee asked to which position he had been promoted. At this the departmental head asked the employee in which position he was currently working? The head was astonished to know that the poor employee who had been working in the organization for the past two years had not even been issued an appointment letter and was unaware of his designation.

When the employee tried to get his appointment letter issued from the HRD department he was ridiculed and asked what was the urgency of getting the appointment letter when he had already worked in the company for two years?

How insecure employees must have felt in this company! This instance speaks volumes of the efficiency of the HRD department and their will and inclination to promote the employee's welfare as well as development of human resources.

The HRD department of such companies should make a determined effort in order to develop a team of satisfied employees. Else, where is the need to have such an inefficient HRD department which is unaware of the job and the purpose the department has been created for? This kind of HRD should be termed Human Resources Deterrent instead of Human Resources Development.

In these companies pendency of work is very high and many files which require urgent action instead keep attracting dust and curse their fate. New entrants in these companies join out of sheer necessity and start their new job under tremendous pressure since they are expected to tie up the loose ends, which were left extremely loose by their predecessors.

They work under tremendous stress and are often reprimanded by the boss for not completing the task within the timeframe because of the pending work and decide to quit due to pressure or due to the high expectations of the demanding boss and the files await their clearance from another new entrant.

The higher the employee turnover in the organization lower the self esteem of the organization itself.

Some companies are not able to retain talented employees due to higher pay packets offered by the competitors and let the employees quit and after a year or so when the employees send a signal to rejoin the organization, they are embraced with open arms with higher pay packets than they were drawing from the competitors and in the process the company earns the ill will of the loyal employees.

These organizations rejoice the return of their disloyal employees by taking the management for yet another ride by announcing that the culture of the organization is excellent and the employees have shown a will to rejoin due to the bad culture prevailing in the competitor's company. In the process they have not only earned the ill will of their existing employees but have shown them a way to get better emoluments in their existing company i.e. by leaving the company for some time and thereafter returning to the company with higher emoluments.

We should try to retain loyal employees by giving them tangible/intangible benefits off and on. And if the employee still quits then never ever take the disloyal employee back.

The organizations who may not have been bestowed with the Almighty's gift of having talented employees then need to develop their employees through class room training sessions and also vigorous follow up through on the job training when a competent supervisor accompanies the trainee to the marketplace and gives demos and shows them how to get the results in the market. This is also termed as mentoring.

During the initial phase of a selling career, mentoring plays a significant role in ensuring that the newcomer follows the right track and does not get swayed by his own immature thoughts and lost in the battlefield i.e. market. Good habits need to be cultivated at the initial stage of one's career. It is extremely difficult to change habits at a later stage in life hence there is a greater need to imbibe good habits in one's personality in the beginning of one's career.

The same holds true for the employees in the production, finance, quality and the other departments. Here the competency level of the trainer comes into picture. Training needs to develop the employee to a level till the time the employee acquires the major skills imparted to him by the trainer and is so well motivated that he wants to rush to the workplace and apply the skills in order to gauge the power of the acquired skills.

To Invest or Not to Invest in Employees

Many companies lack the resources to employ talented persons since they are not in a position to match the pay packets being offered by the competition. These companies need to pump in more money to build up their human resources instead of hiring persons of doubtful backgrounds or hiring a talented employee by offering peanuts.

The employee may join since he/she is need of a job but will ditch the company in a short span and jump the ship to join a competitor where the pay packet is attractive. Do not hire for the sake of hiring and showing to the board of directors that all the vacancies have been filled by talented/non-talented or competent/non competent employees.

The investments made by the organization in its employees yield high ROIs (Return on Investments), contrary to the belief that these investments are futile and a mere wastage of money.

If we offer peanuts we will get only monkeys. Invest in competent employees and reap the benefits in the long run.

Either we initiate processes to make the employees competent by imparting appropriate training and then have a genuine will to retain these comfortable and competent employees or we shall be caught in the vicious cycles of hiring and firing or hiring and not retaining, resulting in high employee turnover rate. Employee turnover is a great obstacle in the progress of many companies who may not understand the employees' needs and or don't fulfil their needs and do not help in the realization of their dreams.

Respect the employee's efforts even if the desired results have not been achieved which may happen once in a while even when the employee had worked with dedication, and sooner or later the employee shall develop respect and attitude to achieve the corporate ambitious goals.

The culprit in the above are the **all-knowing managers** who are trusted highly by the employers who seldom come to know of the exact situations since these sycophants do not want the higher ups to know what exactly is happening in the organization. These kinds of pretenders need to be taken care of and should be discarded directly or indirectly. The earlier this is done the better it is for the overall success of the company.

Over the years some companies may have retained this kind of inefficient employees and may have been suffering due to their wrong and selfish decisions and in turn jeopardizing the welfare of the employees in general and the organization in particular. These organizations are in an urgent need of overhauling and restructuring and should have initiated the process **yesterday**.

Identify these elements and show them that you mean business which is a give and take policy. If they are not contributing to the prosperity of the organization then they need to be shown the door. Get rid of them and utilize the funds so saved to make the grassroots level employees more comfortable and productive.

Multitasking—Pros and Cons

Multitasking is in practice these days in many organizations and has its own pros and cons. The organizations which practice multitasking tend to save on manpower, but only temporarily, since the employee is expected to be an all-rounder.

The point to be pondered upon is: Are employees who are multitasking being compensated adequately for their inputs which include longer working hours and performing multi skill activities? The employees who are used for multitasking have to be highly competent and talented since they are required to perform actions of quantity catching up with quality.

In case the employee is being compensated with both tangible and intangible benefits the employee may go on performing the various tasks. Whereas in some organizations the employees are coerced to undertake multitasking without adequate compensations and in turn the employee is not able to bear the pressure anymore and may ultimately quit which is not a good sign.

Multitasking also leads to employees committing mistakes every now and then and being reprimanded by the boss for the mistakes and in turn the employee becomes dejected and is demoralized. The all-knowing managers in such organizations highlight the mistakes and make it a point so that the employee quits or is made to quit thus increasing their muscle power.

Multitasking in some organizations is practiced in order to save expenses by recruitments of fewer number of employees and showing to the board of directors the savings made by this useless and immature action which is not correct and proves detrimental to the growth of the organization in the long run having a high turnover rate of the employees and in the process the organization itself may create a bad market image.

Such organizations are termed unstable organizations and may not be able to attract talent or retain the talents recruited. These organizations are dreaded by new entrants for their Hire and Fire approach.

Multitasking without adequate compensations makes the employee unsatisfied and he ultimately quits or is made to quit the company due to the extreme work pressure and inadequate compensations.

Recruitment of Recommended Candidates

A company was known to employ only those candidates recommended by higher ups in the organizational hierarchy. This is termed as *sifarishi bharti*.

A study revealed that usually these *sifarishi* candidates who are recommended by higher ups under the pressure of bureaucrats or due to other reasons are usually not talented. Since they are not competent enough to win the positions on their own merits, they make a back door entry by getting recommendation from an influential source and usually end up getting the job.

These *sifarshi* candidates are known to become parasites in the organization since they cannot be sacked in spite of their incompetence as the recommender insists on their retention and the organization has to hold on to these candidates. This becomes a hindrance in the growth of the organization since the higher ups prefer to recruit *sifarshi* employees in order to increase their muscle power in the organization. These *sifarshi* employees owe their loyalties to individuals i.e. to their big uncles and care two hoots for the progress of the organization which was the very purpose of their recruitment.

Recommended candidates by higher ups in the company how so ever incompetent grow under the shelter of their big uncles and keep growing in the company by sucking the blood of efficient workers and ultimately efficient workers quit or are made to quit the organization which is not good.

Chapter Eight

Push or Pull

Everyone thinks of changing the world but no one thinks of changing himself

– Leo Tolstoy

Bura jo dhekan mein chala

Bura na dheeka koi

Jo mun khoja Apna

Mujh se bura na koi

I went in search of finding faults in others.

But realized that there is no person as bad as myself.

Therefore we should search within and improve our own weakness and faults instead of finding faults in others. Be the change we want to see in others. First and foremost we got to change ourselves which may then be emulated by others and they too may change in the process.

Set an example for the team members, friends, peers, subordinates, and bosses so that in the process they start respecting our point of view and may change in the process. We either influence the thought process of others or get influenced by the thought process of others.

Throw Challenge and Push

Always throw a challenge to competent employees and support them in the accomplishment of the desired **goals** which they shall achieve after they have been provided the clarity of the goals to be achieved. The support or **the push** in this case is of **utmost** importance as in the absence of push even competent employees will become incompetent.

When a challenge is thrown to competent employees and the bosses instead of **push** use the **pull** approach, not only will the results not be achieved but the employees may start doubting their own competency levels and are liable to become casual and non-competitive in the long run which is detrimental to any business.

Throw challenges to competitive employees and give a push and see the goals accomplished within the timeframe and find the employees highly motivated ever ready to accomplish more challenges.

Quote their examples in the meetings so that not only do these competitive employees become more competitive but in the process some of the non-competitive employees too progress on the rung of competency. **A comfortable competent employee is a precious asset in any organization**.

The idiot had a knack of writing creative letters and wrote a very creative letter to the divisional office communicating the **grand success** of the company's newly launched product Merck Enzyme vis-à-vis the competitor's enzymes, in the format of zodiac signs wherein the competitive brands were allocated one zodiac sign each. Immediately a telegram (which was the only media of sending important messages in those days i.e. mid seventies) congratulating the idiot for this rare piece of creative work was received from his divisional manager Mr. Vijay Kumar. This motivated the idiot and till date he keeps writing creative letters and reports and of course has preserved the telegram for more than 30 years.

The idiot had a knack of selling non-selling products of the company and created a record sale of Orheptal Tonic which was not only a non-selling but was made fun of by other medical representatives in the company. The idiot took the challenge to sell this tonic and made very good sale. Immediately, a circular was issued by the Divisional Manager titled—*A Newcomer Beats the Stalwarts of Northern Division* which motivated the idiot all the more and even after thirty long years selling of poor selling products has become a habit with the idiot.

In the times to come the idiot bagged three gold tie pins for achieving spectacular sales for three years and stays highly motivated and energetic even today at the young age of 58 years.

Had the idiot not got the **Push** or **Appreciation** from the divisional manager when he had just joined the company in the form of a congratulatory telegram and an appreciation circular from the divisional office he may not have been what he is today—an idiot!

We have abundant resources of appreciation, thank you and sorry within us which is well known to everyone but we become very stingy while using these resources.

We also have resources of criticism and we try to use much more than the quota allocated to us.

Therefore we should try to exhaust all the quota of positives i.e. appreciation, thank you and sorrys and try to return the limited quota of criticisms to the Almighty. When these positives resources are available in abundance why then are we scared to use these?

There are two reasons for this (a) EGO (b) IGNORANCE. EGO is Edging God Off. It is only due to our elephantine egos that we are scared and our ego is hurt when we appreciate somebody or say thank you or sorry. Use these three words frequently and we can see the visible change what take place within us or the person whom we shower with these words.

We are all human beings and should respect one another. He or she may be a peon or the top boss of the company. Heaven will not fall if we call the peon or the driver by name with a prefix Mr? Heaven will not fall if we reciprocate the greetings of a peon or an average employee of the company with warmth? Heaven will not fall if we greet a peon or a subordinate instead of waiting to be greeted by them?

Someone conducted a meeting of the peons to know how they can be motivated and respond positively to any command. The unanimous answer was the command should be in a polite manner since harsh commands are usually resisted to and are not obeyed and may create an unpleasant situation. If we hire the taxi and try to know the taxi driver's name and address him by his name he will start respecting us since we have given him due importance.

Respect Begets Respect

Obviously, if we respect the feelings and sentiments of other human beings our own sentiments and feelings will also be respected by others. A small thank you note sent in time or a sorry communicated timely makes a vast difference. For saying thank you if we take two days to decide and then send a beautifully worded letter of thanks it may not serve the desired purpose than to sms or telephone immediately. Ignorance is not knowing and the remedy for ignorance is learning from books, internet or by interaction with other human beings. An all-knowing person develops an elephantine ego and is not open to new ideas he can neither give new ideas nor can he appreciate new ideas.

The idiot's chairman in the present organization i.e. Pearl Drinks Limited has been providing the desired **push** to the idiot and could get the best out of the idiot and helped the idiot in the best possible way by providing all support.

The idiot started as a novice to head the pet division of the company. The idiot had not seen a PET preform and saw it the first time after he was fortunately selected to head the division without any knowledge of the PET industry and could not sell even a single preform in the first month in spite of his best efforts. But he kept learning about the PET industry and kept trying. PET preforms are test tube like structures made of plastic which are used to make plastic bottles by heating and then blowing in the blowing machines.

Today the idiot can boast of selling 1200 truck loads in a year and has become an authority to reckon with after having acquired the desired information through his initiatives and as on date the idiot has given five presentations regarding the PET Industry in India and abroad i.e. in Dubai and Munich which were par excellence and had been appreciated and applauded by one and all for the contents and powerful presentation.

The best day in the idiot's life was when he gave a powerful presentation in Germany which was attended by his chairman and other directors of the company and appreciation showered by the chairman, "I am impressed, Mr Idiot", still echoes in the mind, rather soul, of the idiot who not only realized his dream of going to Germany but could give an impressive presentation which is the result of the push by the chairman.

Encourage competent employees to perform better by providing the desired support and a little push.

Incidentally the idiot's faith in Linda Goodman's *Sun Signs* has strengthened all the more since he has developed an immense belief that Scorpios have the knack of getting the best out of him/others with their personal charm and proper handling of the rare commodity i.e. employees.

By using yesterday's method today we will not be in business tomorrow.

Human minds and parachutes work only when they are open. A parachute if not open will result in a major casualty and even death. Similarly, the human mind if not open will be closed forever and will make the person incompetent forever.

TORI Window

T—TRUST

O—OPENESS

R—RELIABILITY

I—INTERDEPENDENCE

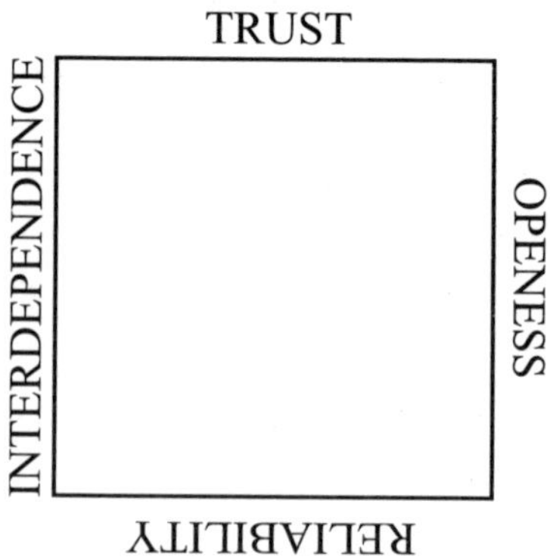

Interpersonal skills need to be developed by broadening the TORI window.

One should trust others and the more we trust others, the more they in turn shall trust us and better the relationship. One should open up. The more the openness, the better the trust and the healthier the relationship. Similarly, the reliability and interdependence among superiors, peers, subordinates, family and friends needs to be broadened.

Persons with a broader TORI Window are the people who trust others and others trust them. They open up before others and others reciprocate in the same spirits, thus building long-lasting relationships, whether on the personal or professional levels. These people are respected professionally, personally as well as in society. People with a broader TORI Window only do good to others. They seldom speak ill of any situation or person under any circumstance.

They are respected, trusted and are emulated by others for their positive traits.

Chapter Nine

Encouragement—a Big Source of Inspiration

The Story of Two Frogs

Two frogs fell into a well accidentally and started shouting for help. Others frogs tried their level best to pull their friends out of the well but did not succeed in their efforts. Meanwhile the frogs in the well started jumping up and down in order to get out of the well. The frogs on top of the well yelled to the frogs inside the well that they should stop trying otherwise they will bleed to death.

One frog finally gave up the efforts and died out of exhaustion and haemorrhage but the other frog did not give up but kept jumping with more energy in spite of the fact that the frogs on top of the well were trying to dissuade him by yelling again and again to die quietly in the well and not to keep jumping.

Ultimately, in spite of the shouting and yelling the frog could take a long leap and came out of the well. All the frogs waiting outside the well were astonished how this frog managed to come out of the well which was virtually an impossible task. Other frogs were astonished to know that the frog which came out of the well was deaf and was thinking that the other frogs were cheering him up and were encouraging him to come out of the well. The mistaken encouragement proved a blessing in disguise and the frog emerged victorious.

Encouragement is a great source of inspiration.

Appreciate in the Open and Criticize In Camera

In order to inspire your team keep on encouraging the team members. Always appreciate the team member in open i.e. in front of the other team members whereas when you want to reprimand someone for doing something wrong do it in isolation. With this kind of approach one can build a cohesive and a winning team when the morale of the team players will be at the highest.

Usually it is seen that some immature managers discourage team members in the open criticizing them every now and then and never ever appreciate the team work or team member and ultimately end up having a demoralized team.

Open criticism is very dangerous as it has a multiple effect. The idiot is of the view that in case the boss abuses a team member in camera the team member may, sooner or later, forget it; but if done in front of ten team members its repercussions shall be ten times. The team member shall feel humiliated in front of his colleagues. There may be five members of the team who may be good buddies of the abused team members and later on they shall come to rescue of their buddy. They may eventually get divided into two teams and these five buddies may develop an aversion to such a stupid team leader and in turn this team leader may lose the respect from the team members. Whereas the same abuse can be absorbed by the team member in case the team leader had the maturity to criticize in camera i.e.in isolation.

Idiot is not advocating never ever scold the team members in open but this should be done in case the team leader in spite of personal counselling to an erring team member for at least five occasions, fails to achieve the desired performance. He should then intimidate the erring and warn team member by saying that next time he shall scold the erring member in open. When condemning in open he should declare that this is being done in spite of personal counselling on earlier five occasions and believe it the rest of the team may come to the rescue of the team leader and may start putting in their own efforts in order to improve the erring team member. The team shall develop greater respect for the leader.

Be Own Encouragers

There are moments in life when you find things not moving the way you want, when the negative emotions are predominant. These are known as the gloomy days or the ups and downs in life and that is the period when you need to shed all the negative thoughts by the positive ones. During these moments, 'Be your own encouragers'.

Go through the memories of the happy days, your successes, your accomplishments which you may have stored in the form of photographs in albums, inspirational and appreciation letters you may have received on earlier occasions.

Read inspirational and motivating books and watch movies which you like the most. Try to take a short break from the routine and spend time with close friends and members of the family who have a positive influence on you and believe it, **this works**.

During the gloomy days you are the Lord Hanuman who is ignorant of the supernatural powers you have been bestowed with and your inner self needs to remind you of your great powers. Once encouraged from within you once again start performing Mind Boggling Actions and emerge victorious.

Chapter Ten

Dream and Drive

People who dream in the night
See them go into vanity
People who dream with their eyes open
Often make them into a reality.
There are three kinds of persons:

1. The Ones Who Do Not Dream At All

These people either do not have the time to dream or are so averse to dreaming and they do not have any objective in life and are complacent with whatever the Almighty has offered. They are not believers in the karma theory i.e. Do your best and leave the rest. One should go on and on performing our karma and should not unnecessarily worry about the fruits of our labour, which will be taken care of by The Almighty.

Such people are usually very casual and often have negative emotions and thoughts. They develop a feeling that neither are they okay and nor is the world around them. They find this world a terrible place to live in and also the organization they are in, a terrible organization to work for.

These kinds of people see only the negatives in all situations, persons and circumstances.

2. Those Who Dream But Do Not Act At All

These kind of persons are experts in building castles in the air and want to live there, but since the castles are not there they keep living as they are. These people only dream of doing great things but do not put any effort to realize their dreams. These people want to have the cake and eat it too.

Example: One such person was carrying a basket full of eggs from his village to the town to sell the eggs. On the way, he got tired and wanted to take rest under the shade of a tree. He kept the basket full of eggs, and took a nap to refresh himself.

Whilst asleep he dreamt that he had sold all the eggs in the town at a very good price and with the money he bought hens. The hens laid more eggs and he sold those eggs too in the market. So, successful was he that he had built a very big poultry farm. He accumulated more and more wealth and got married to a beautiful girl of his village.

He dreamt that they had four children. One of his sons comes to him when he was sleeping and asks him for Rs. 100/- since this son was a spoilt child and used to waste money he was scolded by the father. The angry father kicked his son and told his son to go away in the dream.

In reality, instead of kicking the son, the man kicked the basket full of eggs. In the process, all the eggs broke and he earned nothing out of it. These kind of personalities keep on dreaming throughout their lives and achieve nothing since they do not act at all.

3. Persons Who Dream Big and Pursue Their Dream Making it a Reality

This class is a rare class. This class initiates a project and then pursues it all life long; they are not afraid of their repeated failures since the project was started with a firm conviction and patient planning and above all with mind blowing actions which they pursued with conviction.

To name a few personalities in this class: Dr APJ Kalam, Dr Manmohan Singh, Mr. Sachin Tendulkar, Mr MS Dhoni, Mr Virender Sehwag, Mrs Kiran Bedi, Ms. Lata Mangeshkar, Mr AR Rehman and many others.

Imagine the efforts they must have put in order to drive their dreams. The number of hours they may have practiced to achieve proficiency and perfection in their fields. What a tremendous focus they possessed and what commitment to excel in their untiring efforts. They are celebrities today, not accidentally but because they planned their success by driving their dreams to an extent that it became a reality.

There are persons who live to eat whereas there is yet another class who eat to live. Of course the later class is better than the former since the later class remains healthy physically as well as tough mentally and this is the class who usually dream and drive the dream to an extent that the dreams are realized and the dreamer gets a sense of fulfilment and satisfaction.

Similarly there are people who live to work and the other class is the persons who work to live. Here the former is relatively a much better option than the later. The persons who work to live are the people who are forced to do their jobs or business for mere survival and they are contented with whatever they earn in the process. These people may dream which usually they do not but they will never ever drive the dream further and may stop dreaming altogether one day.

The persons who live to work are the persons who are passionate about their jobs, their business, their studies, their learning and applications of the learnings and their hobbies; hence whatever they do, they do with convictions and once convinced within then they leave no stone unturned in order to drive their dream to such an extent that it becomes a reality. They are satisfied internally after they proudly achieve what they did drive with excellence of efforts. This class is full of enthusiasm and is always positive in their attitude and the very positive in their approach towards life.

Chapter Eleven

Mr Shine or Mr Survive

I will not say I faltered 1000 times. I will say that I discovered that there are 1000 ways that can cause failure

– Thomas Edison

One should be very clear in one's mind what kind of future we are looking to? Some people are satisfied in only making two ends meet and earn a reasonable salary. Nothing interests much to these type of people since they are contented with whatever they are getting and believe in the theory: You will keep on getting what you are getting till you keep on doing what you are doing.

Do Better and Get Better

The above kind of personalities are usually found in government offices and public sector undertakings where it is mainly the entry which is difficult and thereafter we may or may not contribute much, still we keep on enjoying the cozy comforts of our so called job and are likely to have a closed mindset which may not be open to implement new ideas and may jeopardize the organization by calling for strikes every now and then. This kind of people, instead of contributing to the success of the organization, are more concerned with their own welfare. These types of people usually retire mentally much earlier than their physical retirement.

This class is usually busy discussing bonus, ex-gratia, gratuity, pay commission reports, and arrears. This class of people also sometimes sets objectives which they may start enthusiastically but within a short span they quit trying since they started without any conviction and usually do not have a well defined plan of action to be implemented.

Mr. Shine is a different class altogether. You will find them enthusiastically chatting with their colleagues and usually found very busy at the workplace.

This class of employees are dreamers and are result oriented. They set objectives for themselves and they make a plan to implement to achieve these objectives in a well defined timeframe. They may not be always successful in reaching their objectives but they leave no stone unturned and put untiring efforts and above all a focused approach.

After they achieve one objective they set another objective and implement their well planned efforts in order to achieve their objectives. They dream of their success and perform actions of excellence no sooner do they start a task and always have a positive attitude. This kind of people have their own style of functioning which others too try to follow.

This class develops good habits and is well dressed and is prepared for any challenge in their professional as well as personal lives. This kind of people usually do not get tired since they are very passionate about what they do and they always enjoy doing it. There are supernatural powers also which help these kinds of persons to forge ahead in their missions.

This class develops a positive aura around them and become great motivators.

The idiot came in contact with **a rare shine class person** Mr. J.C. D'Lima, director Merck India. Immaculately dressed, highly intelligent, full of enthusiasm to face any challenge. In the evening he would be in casuals wearing a highly impressive Charagh Din shirt and an ever smiling face.

Once, in one the parties hosted by the above **Shine** the idiot had a drink or half extra and got a bit sozzled. The **Shine** gave not even the slightest hint since the party was hosted by him at his residence.

In the morning while attending a seminar the idiot met the above Shine in the elevator and greeted him with a very warm, "Good Morning, Sir". The shine replied in a very harsh and sarcastic tone, "Good Morning, Mr Idiot." The idiot apologized for having an extra drink during the previous day's party. The Shine said, "I never ever said a word about the party so why are you repenting?" This indirect Kick in the A?? (KITA) left an unforgettable mark on the idiot's soul. What a sophisticated form of KITA?

A year after the above episode another seminar was organized by the organization and on the final day this same Mr Shine hosted another party at his residence. The idiot participated actively in the deliberations of the seminar and had controlled drinks. While seeing off the guests Mr Shine was at the door wishing everyone a good night in a very refined way. The idiot was highly impressed when Mr. SHINE complimented him saying, "You have a lot of material in you Mr Idiot."

One day the idiot met another Mr Shine i.e. the present chairman of the company he is currently working for. The idiot was late to reach office by one hour. The chairman met him in the elevator and after exchange of pleasantries the chairman gave him a KITA in a beautiful and sophisticated way by asking where he lived. Vikaspuri, Sir. Answered the idiot but could get the indirect message being communicated by the chairman, telling the idiot indirectly that he was late.

In order to reciprocate, the idiot who used to sit late for an hour in the office doing his job, that day sat in the office for two hours extra and returned the KITA in the form a tangible apology. Needless to add, thereafter the idiot used to come well in time to the office.

The chairman in the organization is known for his refined behaviour and who under normal circumstances does not believe in offending the employees with harsh words and pays compliments to the employees every now and then to boost the morale of the employees. There are many employees who have got greatly influenced by the chairman due to his refined behaviour that they do not want to leave the company in spite of opportunities elsewhere.

The idiot worked for another Mr Shine who rose to the position of director in the organization and was extremely popular among his team members as he used to appreciate them every now and then—sometimes for their immaculate dress and sometimes for the qualities possessed by them. The team members used to respect this Mr Shine from the core of their heart. The idiot still maintains a relation with this Mr. Shine and seeks his mature guidance in the hour of need and he is always obliged.

The idiot was invited by this Mr. Shine for dinner at his residence along with his wife and son who was hardly 4 years old then and was crazy about double-decker buses and would insist on being taken on a joyride on them every now and then.

After the dinner the Shine gifted a toy double-decker to the idiot's son. What a well thought gift? The idiot had nothing but appreciation for his boss. Whenever the idiot was assigned a task by this shine he would put his heart and soul into accomplishing the assigned job and usually accomplish it successfully.

The Bigger We Think the Bigger We Achieve

What is the secret of success? Right Decisions!

How do you make right decisions? Experience!

How to get experience? Wrong Decisions!

– Dr APJ Abdul Kalam

Sir Edmund Hillary who conquered Mount Everest along with Sherpa Tensing did not succeed in his initial attempt to reach the peak and returned to the base camp. Nevertheless, his countrymen really appreciated and applauded this kind of rare venture being undertaken by one of their countrymen and wanted to honour Sir Edmund Hillary in public.

Sir Edmund Hillary was called on the dais where there was a huge portrait of Mount Everest and Sir Hillary while addressing the gathering pointed towards the portrait and said, "You cannot grow bigger, but I can certainly think bigger and conquer you." And ultimately Sir Edmund Hillary succeeded in conquering the summit.

The bigger we think the bigger we can achieve. So when a choice to think big or small why not choose the better option i.e. Big..

Chapter Twelve

The Power of Prayers and Blessings

If we cannot love the person whom we can see, how can we love God whom we cannot see?

– Mother Teresa

The late Mother Teresa who even today is the epitome of love and compassion has proved to the world the power of prayer and blessing! She may even be no more on this planet but still rules the hearts of many by the great deeds she performed for the benefit of the humanity.

Prayers and blessings have great powers. In the S.K.Y. meditations one is required to bless everyone, mother, father, guru, brothers, sisters, relatives, friends, and bosses. Peers, subordinates and enemies too, if any. These blessings are returned to us and we are in turn blessed by the positive energies.

By blessing every one we create a highly pious atmosphere. And how can we do bad or think ill of our enemies if we bless them every day? People who practice SKY are known to perform good virtues only and lead a very purposeful life.

Prayers also have tremendous powers. Narrated below is a true incident. This interview appeared in the *Indian Express* dated January 24, 2010.

Malvika Mala Singh, the editor of SEMINAR was interviewed by a French traveller Nadine Kreisberger.

The editor Malavika Mala Singh went to meet Mother Teresa on the insistence of a close friend. Mother Teresa's sharp, clear eyes pierced through the editor and the mother asked, "Do you believe in God and in the power of prayer?" "I had to be honest and said, "I do not really know." She hugged me, told me I was a good woman, not to change, speak my mind and be myself.

Then, out of the blue, she asked what was bothering me? I told her a friend's son had been kidnapped two weeks ago and the situation was desperate. She simply said, "I will prove to you the power of prayer. I will pray all the night with the sisters." The next day Kim was released. As I got home, Mother was on the phone saying, "I have proved to you the power of prayer"

Success and spirituality go hand in hand. We may start by being successful first and end up becoming spiritual as well or we may start with spirituality first and become successful as the end product. Spiritual persons are not only self realized but are bestowed with materialist and professional success as well.

The best way is to practice putting in best efforts and lead a spiritual life so that one is successful in leading a purposeful and successful life. It may not be necessarily success in sales but which ever field we are in it is ultimately the focused efforts which bring about the best of results.

Karma Theory

According to Hindu mythology a person is born with *sanchit karmas* and on this planet earth accumulates innumerable *prarabadh karmas*. *Sanchit karmas* are the karmas which one brings when one is born. And *prarabadh karmas* are accumulated during our evolution and growth on earth.

When we do well to others we ward off the ill effects of our *sanchit karmas* and also by doing good to others we accumulate good Karmas. **Do good to others and good must happen to you sooner or later in some form or another**.

There is the divine in all of us in the form of atman but this divinity within is surrounded by monsters viz. *kaam*, *krodh*, *lobh*, *moh* and *ahankaar* (lust, anger, greed, attachment to worldly pleasures and above all ego).

Once we are successful in getting rid of these evils we become one with the Almighty or the total consciousness. By merging our atman (fractional consciousness) with the Almighty and we become a self-realized person.

All the bad deeds are done due to the aforesaid evil forces surrounding our pure self i.e. atman. Getting rid of these evil forces is the essence of any religion only the methodology is different, the line of action may be different and the very approach may be different but the objective is the same i.e. realization of our pure self atman which once realized illuminates our inner self with the divine power and thereafter one performs only good deeds and becomes realized and the self is illuminated.

Wrong deeds are performed out of ignorance of our inner self blocked by these monsters. For example Besides pious Mount Kailash is the Mansarovar Lake which when is full of ripples can not reflect the image of the sacred Mount Kailash.

The mountain can be viewed only after these ripples of *Kaam*, *Krodh*, *Lobh*, *Moh* and *Ahankaar* are calmed down. In a still Mansarovar Lake one can see the calm and quiet reflection of Mount Kailash.

Here the mind is the Mansarovar Lake and Mount Kailash is God and we can see the reflection of God within us only after we are successful in getting rid of the ripples and have a pure heart through good deeds and karmas.

"When we're unhappy, God smiles at us,

When we're happy, God laughs at us,

But when we make others happy, God salutes us"

– *Charlie Chaplin*

Kisi ki mooskarahato pe ho nissaar

Kisi ka dard mil sakey to le udhar,

Kissi ke vaaste ho tere dil me piyaar

Jeena isi ka naam hai.

When we happily share others' happiness without envy and help others in distress and love others from the core of our heart, this is what an ideal human being is like.

Once Guru Nanak Dev ji went to a village along with his disciples Bala and Mardana. The village was full of crooks, thieves, robbers and other bad elements. After his sermons Guru Nanak Dev Ji blessed the villagers:

Vasde Raho—You should all live in this village happily hereafter.

Thereafter he went to the next village which was full of noble gentle and pious people after the sermons he blessed the villagers:

Ujjar Jaao—You should all leave the village and spread all over the world.

Both Bala and Mardana were perplexed and asked the master why he had given good blessings to bad people and bad blessings (curses) to good people?

Guru Nanak Ji replied, "I have blessed the bad people to stay in a confined place so that they do not influence others with their bad karmas, deeds and evil thoughts. Good people when scattered all over the world will give the message to the world to do good to others, be religious and live the life of an ideal human being by making the world a better place to live."

The crux of the *Guru Granth Sahib* is:

Naam Japo,

Kirit Karo,

Te Wund Chchako

Be religious and practice good virtues, perform your actions with efficiency on this planet and feed the poor in addition to your own family.

By showering appreciation frequently, by using the word thank you often and by saying sorry if we had committed a mistake we will shed our ego. We shall open our mind which can work wonders by generating innovative ideas and strategies. We should not live in our so called shell but with our interactions should develop ourselves as well as others.

If I have one idea and you have one and we do not exchange it then you will have only one idea and I will have only one idea. But if we exchange our ideas we create a win-win situation since both of us will have two ideas each. Therefore the exchange of ideas multiplies and non-exchange makes the idea die in the long run.

Do Good Get Good

Narrated below is a true story:

A farmer by the name of Fleming was ploughing his field. Suddenly, he heard the groan of a child. Fleming ran in the direction from where the voice was coming and saw a child neck deep in mud. The child was crying for help. Fleming did his duty and with great difficulty could pull the child out of the mud. The child thanked him and went away.

Next day when Fleming was ploughing his field a gentlemen approached him. The gentleman told Fleming that he was the father of the child rescued by him the previous day. The gentlemen asked Fleming how he could repay this kindness.

Fleming politely refused to accept anything elaborating that it was his duty which he performed by saving the gentleman's son. Standing besides Fleming was his son. The gentlemen requested Fleming to give him permission so that he can provide the best of education to Fleming's son in the city. To this Fleming agreed reluctantly.

Fleming's son was brought up by the gentlemen and studied in the best of medicine colleges and grew up to become Alexander Fleming—the inventor of penicillin. The gentleman's own son grew up and was hospitalized with an acute attack of pneumonia. Ultimately the gentleman's son got cured by the administration of penicillin which was invented by Alexander Fleming son of Farmer Fleming. This gentleman who was cured of pneumonia was none other than Sir Winston Churchill.

Mysterious Supernatural Power

The idiot had been residing in an air force camp in the suburbs of Delhi. The son of the commanding officer Sh. Om Prakash Sharma became a great buddy of the idiot and they lived in the camp for three years. The name of his friend was Narender Sharma.

Thereafter the idiot's father was transferred to another camp in Delhi where the idiot was admitted to the Air Force Central School. The commanding officer too was transferred to Amritsar. The two friends were thus separated. The idiot as well the commanding officer's son Narender were in touch through letters (the only way of communications in those days) for a couple of years and thereafter there was no communication and the exchange of letters stopped.

In the mean while the idiot did his graduation and pursued pharmacy and became a medical representative and started working in Punjab. The idiot was promoted and was required to cover Amritsar district as well.

One day the idiot was waiting to catch a train at Amritsar railway station and suddenly came across a gentle man who resembled his buddy's father. The idiot approached the gentle man and asked whether he was Sh. Om Prakash Sharma the commanding officer of the Air Force Camp?

The gentle man nodded his head in affirmative and asked the idiot how could he recognize? The commanding officer had seen the idiot fifteen years back when he was studying in 9th class and was a teenager and today he had grown and was a happily married man.

The idiot's told his name and his father's name and the gentleman was surprised to recognize the idiot and asked about the welfare of the other members of the family to which the idiot replied that they were in Bangalore and by the grace of the Almighty are doing well.

The obvious next question the idiot asked the gentleman was, "Sir, How is my buddy Narender?"

"Here is Narender," replied the gentleman and showed a red coloured cotton bag which contained the ashes of his great friend Narender.

A cold chill ran down the idiot's spine after he came to know that his friend Narender had become a flight lieutenant in the air force and was posted in Rajauri in J&K and had met a fatal accident two days back and the father was taking the mortal remains of his son to Haridwar so that the departed soul of his son rests in peace.

How did the idiot come across his friend after a gap of fifteen years is not a mystery but it's the firm belief of the idiot that there certainly exists a **supernatural power** which had ensured that the idiot at least sees his friend Narender who may no longer be alive but pay obeisance to his mortal remains.

The idiot does not have the slightest idea or knowledge regarding the publishing aspect of his maiden attempt of writing a book and was in search of a good publishing house for the publishing of his book, *AN IDIOT WHO SOLD A SHIP*. He had been enquiring from various sources for guidance in this context.

Is it then, merely a coincidence that an article about publishers appeared in the *Times of India* dated February 7, 2010 which has surprisingly featured details pertaining to the leading publishers whom the idiot contacted?

It may be foolish to attribute the above happening to the existence of the Supernatural Power but is it really foolish? Or does there exist a supernatural power which is supporting the idiot's efforts in its own mysterious way and is constantly guiding the idiot.

The idiot had just been nurturing a faint idea to pen down a book one day in his subconscious mind but believes it was this supernatural power who has provided the extraordinary power to undertake this herculean task of writing a book in a very short span of time. In case the book is successful the idiot's faith in the power of the supernatural power and the blessings and praying shall strengthen all the more.

Chapter Thirteen

Happiness and Unhappiness—Only A Mind-set

Do not compare yourself with anyone in this world.

If you do so you are insulting yourself

– Alen Strike

Wrong Comparisons

Once after the Olympics were over, it was found that the athletes who had won the bronze medals were happy but the athletes who had won the silver medals, were disappointed and sad. Further research revealed that the athletes who had won bronze medal considered themselves fortunate compared to the athletes who did not win even a single medal. Whereas, those who won silver medals were comparing themselves with the athletes who had won gold medals.

It is the mindset of people which makes them happy or unhappy, circumstances remaining the same.

When we get up each morning we have a choice to be happy or unhappy during the course of the day. When we have a choice to make, why not to choose the better option, that is happiness?

A Barefooted Man

Once a man was walking barefoot in the scorching sun and was cursing his luck at having to walk barefoot in such hot weather. Suddenly, he saw another man coming from the opposite side of the road, on crutches. He thought to himself, "What a great tragedy that man has undergone? I at least have legs, so what if I do not have shoes to wear.

God has already bestowed us the privileges we deserve and not the ones we desire. To achieve what we desire one has to put in the best of efforts. One should have smaller needs and desires and should have a sense of self contentment. Everybody cannot get everything that he desires. Compromises need to be made at various levels in order to live a blissful life.

If we think that it is only the rich who are happy and not the poor, then we are wrong. The rich may have wealth but may not have a heart to spend and may go on accumulating wealth, in the end leaving everything behind when they die. The story goes that Alexander the Great had instructed that when he dies his hands should be kept open with the palms facing the sky so that everybody learnt that we all have to go empty handed after death which is the truth of human life.

Ants Act Whereas Crabs Crib

If you put 10 crabs in a jar, all the crabs throughout their lives will remain in the jar because whenever one crab will try to come out of the jar another crab will pull him down.

Whereas if we put ants in a jar, one ant will initiate the process of coming out of the jar and other ants will follow the leader ant and will come out of the jar forming a line. We therefore should not act as crabs in a team but try to emulate the ant example.

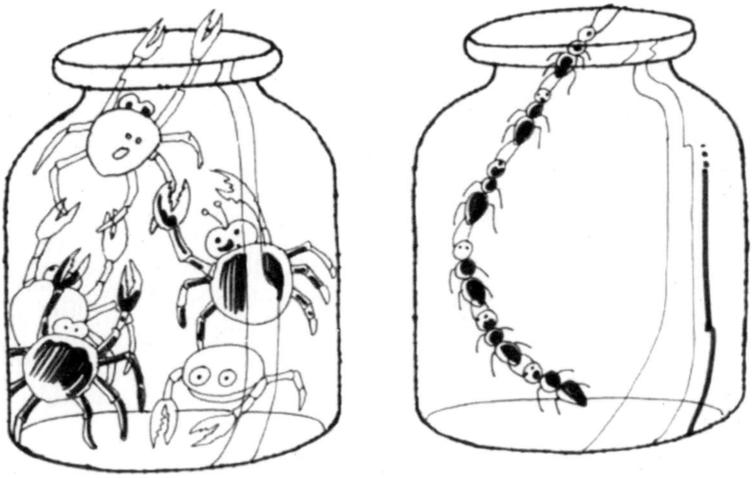

Crabs crib but the Ants act

Smile as Often as Possible

The major difference between human beings and animals is—human beings can smile whereas animals cannot. It is said one is incompletely dressed if one is not wearing a smile. A smile is a rare virtue bestowed upon human beings by the Almighty and should be used frequently. A smile at the right movement makes the other individual return the smile and the environment created by the smile is lighter and individuals who smile often are liked by society.

Whereas people like to keep a distance from individuals who are usually found frowning. While smiling we use nine muscles of our face whereas while frowning we use 39 muscles. Therefore, where is the need to waste the energy of 39 muscles and create a tense atmosphere when using only 9 muscles creates a positive and lighter environment?

Smile often and pass on this contagious infection to others in society so that the whole society smiles.

Vishal Don't!

We bring up our children and teach them many things. Parents, out of frustration, scold and even slap their children. They think this is the best way to bring up the child. We often scold by yelling, "Vishal don't touch the television, Vishal don't go out of the room, Vishal don't come in kitchen... Ultimately when Vishal is admitted to school and upon being asked his name by the teacher, Vishal replies, "Vishal Don't" (so used is he to hearing the word repeatedly from his parents!)

We should therefore bring up our children in a congenial and free atmosphere and we should explain to the child, why he should not do this or that, without yelling. By yelling the parents not only waste their energy but also hamper the mental and physical growth of the child.

Invoke the power of hanuman of the team

There are three traits in any individual:

A. Parent

B. Adult

C. Child (Little Master)

The parent in an individual always calls for security, protection, affection and respect and provides guidance.

The adult in an individual is the maturity which makes the individual analyze situations and circumstances and prompts the person to act in a right way and right direction.

The Child (Little Master): There is a child in every individual. This child (Little Master) element in the personality of the individual provides enthusiasm, love, innocence, passion, creativity and freedom to perform any action as per individual's desires.

When the child element in the personality is dominant, well protected by the parent and adult element, it gives shape to an enthusiastic, positive, creative, loving and affectionate analyzing and mature individual. Try to encourage the child element of your own self as well as that of others.

Lord Hanuman had many powers in him which was a boon by the Almighty. He had so much power and potential that he could fly in the air and strength that he could carry a mountain with his hands. And he had the power to shrink or expand his size beyond any limits. In the *Ramayana* Lord Hanuman flew over and crossed the ocean to reach Lanka in search of Mata Sita. He brought the whole mountain since he was not able identify the sanjeevini herb which was a cure for an unconscious Lakshman.

INVOKE THE HIDDEN TALENT OF THE TEAM MEMBERS

It is said that these supernatural powers needed to be evoked and could be done only when someone reminded Lord Hanuman that he is bestowed with the supernatural powers and time has come to use the same for the accomplishment of the task and these powers needs to be used. Without this reminder Lord Hanuman was an ordinary human being.

Similar are the strengths possessed by the team members. The idiot is not saying you should tell a team member to cross the sea by flying and land in Lanka but always try and appreciate the positive qualities of all the individuals in the team and motivate them to use their strengths overlooking their weakness for the realization of the team objectives.

Remind them again and again of their past achievements and make them believe that they have the capability and competence to achieve the desired results. In case you start calling a duffer a wise man, he initially may not believe it and may be taken aback at such a revelation. In the process he will wonder whether there may be an iota of truth in the statement; then may start behaving as a wise man and may eventually become a wise man. Tell a thief that he is honest and in turn there may be a time when he stops stealing altogether or at least he shall act honest in front of you.

Nevertheless recognize the positives traits of your team members, keep on encouraging them that they have the potential, keep on showering genuine compliments now and then and ultimately the team shall develop a **belief** of their strengths and they in turn shall face any challenge boldly. At times when the team is not able to deliver results, at least appreciate the efforts put in by the members to keep their morale high. We will be able to develop a highly motivated and cohesive team. This team may have lost a battle but shall win the war.

A poor man who religiously served a sadhu was asked by the sage to make a wish which the sage would help to fulfill. The poor fellow said he wanted to be happy. The sage asked the poor fellow to get the shirt of the happiest person he comes across.

The poor man started his mission of searching the happiest man. Thinking the rich are very happy he first tried to meet all the rich persons but to his dismay he found that although they had enough wealth they were not happy due to one reason or another.

For many days he did not come across a single happy person. Suddenly he heard the humming of a happy song which was coming from the top of a tree. He saw a man cutting the wood and humming a beautiful song of happiness. The poor man then asked the woodcutter to come down from the tree and the man came down.

"Are You Happy?"

"Yes of course I am very happy."

"Kindly give me your shirt for a day."

"But I do not have a shirt!"

Someone may not be happy even after having two dozen shirts but another may be very happy with just one shirt.

Happiness is only a state of mind. One can be happy under any circumstances—favourable as well as unfavourable.

Money can buy us innumerable delicacies to eat but not the appetite to eat. Money can buy us a very comfortable bed but we cannot buy sleep with money. Money can buy us a big bungalow with many floors which will only remain a **house**. And on the other hand a **home** how so ever small may have the warmth of the family members of a closely knit family who may be far happier than the family in a palacious **house** who are insensitive to the feeling of one another.

In our life we should love people and use things; but we have started loving things and using people to our advantage.

Chapter Fourteen

True Friends—a Rare Gift

Awards become corroded,

Friends gather no dust.

– Jesse Owens

F-Few

R-Relations

I-In

E-Earth

N-Never

D-Die

We should count our age not by the number of years but by the number of friends we have made. Still better by the number of years we have been able to retain the true friends.

True and loyal friends are a great asset to any individual. In true friendship it is a give and take relationship which sustains over very long periods. True friendship develops when the feeling to give is more than the craving to take. True friendship develops when you accept another individual with all his negative as well as positive qualities.

Incidentally, the idiot has a friend wherein the relationship has not only survived but has strengthened in the last 42 years. The idiot once made a new year greeting card with his own hands and painted a picture of a rose which was illuminated by sprinkling shining powder on it. Then the idiot made an envelope by himself and took the card and cycled seven kilometres to his friend's house. Such was the love, affection, innocence in the relationship.

The friend has preserved the greeting card for the last 42 years which they both see at times to reminiscence the old memories strengthening their friendship bond further. The idiot's daughter was hospitalized for three months in Delhi and this friend would visit the hospital around 11.30 pm. every alternate day, covering a distance of almost 30 kms on his scooter. He used to leave the hospital for work around 6 am in the morning after having a nap of 2-3 hours on a vacant hospital stretcher.

The idiot had another friend who used to spend 50% of his salary for buying books of great authors. He was a voracious reader. Once this friend along with the idiot was sitting in a group of friends and one fellow of the group was being mocked at and pulled up merely out of fun. This friend goes to the kitchen and prepares seven cups of tea. Incidentally, a fly fell in one of the cups. The idiot was watching the whole episode when his friend was engrossed in preparing tea unaware that he is being watched. The friend took out the dead fly out of the tea and idiot thought that this cup will be given to the friend who was being pulled up by the group. To his bewilderment that cup of tea from which the dead fly was taken out was kept for himself by the friend who prepared the tea and rest six cups were served to others.

The idiot would not like to boast of his many other friends whom he has retained for the past more than three decades.

Chapter Fifteen

Forget and Forgive

Jo toko kaanta boovae

Taahi boovae tu phool

Toko to phool ke phool hein

Vaako hae trishool

When someone plants thorns for you

You should plant flowers to him.

In return you will get flowers

And he will get thorns.

Such are the wonderful ways of nature.

If someone does bad to you, you should not react by doing bad but instead keep on doing good. Sooner or later you will get in return the good and the bad shall go to the fellow who has done bad to you—so runs the law of nature from which there is no escape.

When someone does bad to us it should be written on the sand and when something good is done to us then it should written on stone. We should try to forget whatever bad has happened to us and try to forgive the guilty and when someone has done something good to us then we should try to reciprocate by doing good to the individual or may be the society at large. Imagine if all the inhabitant start practicing these virtues; won't this world be a better place to live?

Consider Priyanka Gandhi's compassion in going to the jail in Vellore to meet Nalini Sriharan the women who conspired to kill her father Late Shri Rajiv Gandhi. Both Sonia and Priyanka Gandhi have pleaded that the death sentence of Nalini be commuted to life imprisonment. What a magnanimous gesture on the part of the Gandhi family?

Take the example of Alexander the great King who pardoned the captive King Porus and acceded to his request that he be treated as one king treats another. The generous Alexander treated a captured enemy with respect and dignity.

Jaako rakhey saaieya,

Maar sakey na koye

Baal na banka kar sakey,

Jo jag beiree hoye.

No one can do any harm to the one who is protected by the Almighty. Even if the entire world is against such a person, he shall emerge victorious without even a single bruise.

The idiot had a servant, let's call him Mr X, who was a spoiled brat and came in contact with the idiot's family through a friend. The idiot's family is very religious. Satsang is conducted in the idiot's house every afternoon.

This Mr. X had been carrying out petty juvenile thefts i.e. removing the bolts from the parked cars and selling the same and making money. From the idiot's house also he stole approximately Rs 4000/- in a span of one month—not in one go but intelligently in instalments.

This was discovered after a month and Mr. X confessed to having stolen the money. Mr. X's father who was a cook in a restaurant in Delhi was summoned and he agreed to repay the stolen amount in instalments of Rs 500/- every month.

Mr. X could have been handed over to the police and could have become a hard core criminal with the ill treatment in the police station or may have been put in Tihar Jail where he would have come in contact with other criminals who would have given beautiful shape to his inner criminal instincts.

Instead the family decided to give him another chance and Mr. X continued serving in our house. His father stuck to his words and returned Rs. 3500/- out of the total Rs 4000/- since the family agreed to provide a rebate of Rs. 500/- in view of the confession made by Mr. X.

After this episode Mr. X served in the idiot's house for another 3-4 years more like a family member than as a servant and took the job of a cook in the restaurant where his father worked. Mr. X kept changing jobs as a cook but used to come to the idiot's house frequently and stay with them. His mother, sister and brother also used to come to our house for satsang.

Today Mr. X's father is happily employed as a cook in Germany for the past four years. And believe it or not, Mr. X is employed in a hotel in Hong Kong for the past four years and keeps calling the idiot over telephone every now and then. He addresses the idiot as Maussa ji, the idiot's wife as Moussi ji and my son and daughter as Bhaiya and Didi. Recently he gave some amount as loan to the idiot's family when some money was required and of course it has been paid back to him.

Imagine what Mr. X had been had he not come in touch with the idiot's family which practiced Gandhigiri and reformed a criminal out of sheer compassion.

The idiot is not advocating that you employ criminals as servants and reform them. But do try to be compassionate towards others and let the process continue. It may help another Mr. X to be employed in Hong Kong and in turn you may get a lifelong so called relative and well wisher and strengthen the chains of humanity.

Chapter Sixteen

The Power of One

The power of one is the power of an individual, team, organization or may be of the total industry as such. This power of one should be increased by putting in various efforts at all levels.

1. One should have one objective every day.
2. One should do one good deed every day.
3. One should take blessings of our parents every day.
4. One should thank the Almighty for giving us this human body every day.
5. One should daily thank the Almighty for whatever has been provided to us by His grace.
6. One should contribute one extra effort for our organization as well the society every day.
7. One should help one's team member or family member every day.
8. One should pray every day.
9. One should look within us every day.
10. One should learn a new English word every day.
11. One should add one new learning every day.

By practicing the above we can feel the difference it shall make in our personal as well as professional lives. We in turn shall start leading a more purposeful life.

We are bound to succeed through the power of one.

GOD is Generator, Operator and destroyer.

GOD is omnipotent, omnipresent and omniscient.

GOD is ONE.

It is a supernatural POWER which is the Static state of THE ALMIGHTY whereas this universe is the dynamic state. In the static state i.e. ABSOLUTE there is energy and consciousness which has the power to become dynamic. This static state is called the SHIVA element and when the energy becomes dynamic it is called the PARVATI element.

Every religion advocates the belief in the power of one THE ALMIGHTY- the methodology may differ. The Hindu worship The Almighty by going to temples and performing various rituals to appease The Almighty. The Muslims go to the Masjids and with the recital of verses from The Sacred Koran wish to be one with The Almighty. The Sikhs visit the gurudwaras and through the pious Granth Sahib worship the Supernatural Power whereas the Christian do this through The Holy Bible and pray in the Churches.

All the religions therefore believe in the Power of One.

Chapter Seventeen

Try and Fail Instead of Not Trying

Winning does not always mean being first.

Winning means you are doing better than you have done before

- Bonnie Blair

Trying and failing is a better option than not trying at all. By not trying we are bound to fail since we have not even tried at all. Trying at least shall ensure that there is a possibility of succeeding. The only negative element of trying is that we may fail. It is only out of fear of failure or non-confidence in one's abilities that we are hesitant to try.

Don't Assume

Thoughts make a vast difference in one's life. One must therefore choose our thoughts carefully since the thoughts become action, which become our habit and ultimately becomes the character. We are the master of our character, so build up a positive attitude and a strong character and attain **success** by trying, trying and trying with conviction; pursue excellence and attain success.

At times we are afraid to appear for an interview since we start nurturing a feeling that we may not fare well and will not be selected for the post. This is a mere **assumption**. These feelings arise out of the negative emotions which should be shed to pave way for the positive emotions. Try to inculcate only positive thoughts and get rid of the negative thoughts.

Negatives thoughts have jeopardized the lives of many and extreme negativity leads to depression and the developments of suicidal tendencies. Why not then remain always positive and full of enthusiasm. When we have a choice to make why not choose to be positive instead of negative.

Everyone is not bestowed with all the privileges in life so one must be content with what we have received from the Lord and not crib about what we do not have. Thank the Lord every day for whatever has been provided to us by His grace.

The idiot during his college days was apprehensive of sitting for the examination and wanted some more time for preparations and wanted to sit the supplementary examinations which were to be held three months later. He obeyed his father's advice of trying and failing and sat for the examination. The idiot not only succeeded in clearing the examination but got distinction in two subjects and was second in his class.

Had the idiot's father not persuaded him to appear for the examination he would have succumbed to his negative emotion and would have embraced defeat without trying.

TRY... try and try and keep trying only then we have a chance to win and will have no regrets later for not trying at all. We come across many people repenting having not tried and they usually curse their luck and try to pass the blame onto others in order to hide their guilt.

Higher the Risk Higher the Reward

Victorious warriors win first and then go to war, while defeated warriors go to war first and then seek to win.

- Sun Tzu

We have got to take calculated risks. Even Sachin Tendulkar has to take risk. **Life itself is a challenge**. And people who make excellence as their motto ultimately succeed in life. One may be born poor but should die rich. Then only will people say he was the fellow who faced the challenge of life boldly and become victorious and not a victim of circumstances. In life we should not be victims but should emerge victorious.

Higher the risk higher the reward. The idiot is not recommending you jump from 10th floor of the building. One would die or get crippled for life.

Calculated risk is the need of the hour. An organization making a profit of 50 crores over revenue of 1000 crores should not shed tears if 50 lacs profit has to be written off on account of bad debts towards the year-end. Instead of not taking the risk and generating a revenue of 900 crores and realizing all the profits of Rs. forty five crores at the year end after taking calculated risk.

Out of the above two situations which is better in today's highly competitive business environment? Most of us will feel the former situation to be a better preposition than the latter. Because in the former the calculated risk was taken and an additional revenue of 100 crores has been achieved with additional profitability of 4.5 crores.

A company which does not take risk has to be contended with lower revenues and lower profits. The same is true about individuals. We have got to take calculated risks to face various challenges posed by circumstances.

An insurance agent was once told by his boss that he had to do a business of five lakhs a day which was an astronomical target since the agent was doing business of not more than two lacs a day. The agent replied, "That it is impossible sir". The boss said, "My dear, see there is possible even in im possible".

The agent went out and returned that evening after procuring a business of seven lakhs and told his boss that to get this business he had to cheat his clients. "But this is immoral," said the boss. The agent said, "Sir, but there is moral in im moral also".

One manager went to attend the tender opening on behalf of his company. The company had been trying unsuccessfully to win the bid for the past two years. This time a bid of approximately 50 crores was won by the company. Whilst returning to office the manager lost his mobile phone and informed his boss that a bid of 50 crores had been won but, "I have lost my mobile phone worth 15 thousand rupees". The boss asked, "What is the link between winning the bid and losing the mobile?" The manager replied, "It is just to inform that I will not be available over mobile for the next one or two days".

After returning to office, the manager went to the boss and said the link between winning the tender and losing the mobile is, "F**or every gain in life we have to lose or sacrifice something.**" In this case the company gained but the employee sacrificed his mobile.

Moral of the story: Be prepared to sacrifice something for every gain in life.

The One-Eyed Nurse

There was a hospital run by Seventh Day Adventists missionaries called Ruby Nelson Hospital. The Medical Superintendent of the hospital was one German doctor, Dr J T Warner who was a very tough guy and most of the medical representatives tried to avoid this particular doctor as he used to meet at very odd hours i.e. after seeing his patients; and he always had a crowd of patients mostly from nearby villages outside his chamber.

There used to be one nurse also who had one artificial eye, and was also averse to medical representatives and used to keep a sharp eye over the medical representatives so that no one sneaked inside the doctor's chamber. After seeing his patients Dr Warner usually used to rush to his residence which was located within the boundary walls of the hospital. When he used to finish seeing the last patient he would just walk out of his chamber and would tell the waiting medical representative, "I do not have time".

The hungry and angry medical representatives used to leave the hospital cursing their fate and of course Dr Warner as well. This hospital had a vast potential to purchase tonics and Dr Warner used to buy one thousand bottles of tonics at a time but was sticking to only one brand for the past many years,

The idiot had a tonic, selling which was a herculean task and other medical representatives of his own company dreaded selling Orheptal which incidentally had an obnoxious odour since it contained liver extract. The idiot decided to sell it to Dr Warner—an impossible task indeed. The idiot believed in the philosophy of trying and failing, instead of not trying at all.

The idiot started on his mission of selling Orheptal to Dr Warner. The first month was lost with the monster nurse glaring at the idiot and Dr Warner usually rushing out of his chamber with words: I do not have time.

It was the peak of summer and the exhausted and frustrated idiot usually returned home after having lunch in a nearby Dhaba as he was a bachelor.

In the second month the idiot told the guarding one eyed nurse that he wants to donate few bottles of Orheptal for the poor patients of Dr Warner. The idiot had piled up a stock of Orheptal samples since none of the other doctors wanted to take the samples such was the image build up by our great tonic Orheptal. But in reality it was a tonic par excellence but the odour of the liver extract could not be masked.

One day the one-eyed nurse took pity on the idiot as she had been seeing him waiting to see Dr Warner on many occasions and the idiot could meet Dr Warner for the first time in his chamber, where he handed over 30 bottles of Orheptal requesting Dr Warner to distribute them among his poor patients. Dr Warner did not budge.

Free bottles were again provided to Dr Warner and strength of the product was highlighted but the doctor remained unmoved.

The idiot in the meanwhile started learning German and could pick up few words initially viz. guten morgen, guten abend, etc.

In the third month the idiot addressed Dr Warner in German, handed over the samples of Orheptal for Dr Warner's poor patients and showed him his German phrase book and told Dr Warner that he has started learning German since he is working for a German MNC Merck and would like Dr Warner to help him in learning German. Lo and behold! Dr Warner readily agreed to the idiots strange request and also gave an order for 1000 bottles of Orheptal. And this order was repeated every month by Dr Warner.

It was a rare achievement in those days and this news reached the managing director who was a German called Comander GKA John. He made it a point to shower appreciation on the idiot for this wonderful achievement during the annual conference in Delhi and also promised to send a personal gift for Dr Warner.

Success is never accidental but is the result of carefully executed planned efforts.

The idiot used to wait for hours to meet the doctor and used to return home disappointed

The Incapacitated Boy Who Became a Judo Champion

This is a story of one 10-year-old boy who decided to learn judo despite the fact that he had lost his left arm in a devastating car accident. Neverthless he never lost his will to put in efforts and believed in failing instead of not trying at all.

The boy began lessons with a judo master. The boy was doing well, so he couldn't understand why, after three months of training, the master had taught him only one move. Master! The boy finally said, "Shouldn't I be learning more moves?"

"This is the only move you know, but this is the only move you'll ever need to know," replied the master. Not quite understanding, but believing in his teacher, the boy kept training.

Several months later, the Master took the boy to his first tournament. Surprising himself, the boy easily won his first two matches. The third match proved to be more difficult, but after some time, his opponent became impatient and charged; the boy deftly used his one move to win the match.

Still amazed by his success, the boy was now in the finals. This time, his opponent was bigger, stronger, and more experienced. For a while, the boy appeared to be overmatched. Concerned that the boy might get hurt the referee wanted to call of the match but decided to continue since the master insisted that the match must continue.

Soon after the match resumed, his opponent made a critical mistake: he dropped his guard. Instantly, the boy used his move to pin him. The boy had won the match and the tournament. He was the champion.

On the way home, the boy and the master reviewed every move in each and every match. Then the boy summoned the courage to ask what was really on his mind. "Sensei, how did I win the tournament with only one move?"

"You won for two reasons," the master answered. "First, you've almost mastered one of the most difficult throws in all of judo. And second, **the only defence for that move is for your opponent to grab your left arm which you don't have.**

Hence in spite of a major handicap the boy tried and succeeded.

Chapter Eighteen

Common Sense Is Not So Common

You are not responsible for what people think of you,

But you are responsible for what you give them to think about you

- Stanly Ferrard

Know the Product

There are some instances where we find commonsense a scare commodity. There are medical representatives who represent pharmaceutical companies and promote the products to the doctors who in turn either buy the products or prescribe the products so that the patient can buy the medicine from the chemist which in turn increases the sale of the company's product.

One such medical representative goes to doctor details (talks about the benefits of the company's product) and towards the end of the talk tells the doctor that the product is very economically priced. The doctor asks the price of the product and the medical representative replies, "Sir, it is a bit costly."—thus condemning his own statement.

Learning: One should be careful while talking to the customers and should not give false statements knowingly or unknowingly.

Do Not Exaggerate

A medical representative goes to a doctor and details his product (in this case an eye drop manufactured by his company which contained sulphacetamide and one more ingredient).

On being asked the use of the additional ingredient by the doctor and not knowing the answer the medical representative replies, "Sir, do you know the use of the additional ingredient?" The doctor answers that he knows but wants to test the medical representative's product knowledge. To this the representative says, "When you know it and I know it, what's the great idea of discussing it?"

Learning: one should know the benefits of our products before we approach the customer to sell the same. One should do our home work well before facing the customers.

Understand the Situation and the Customer

There used to be a medical representative Mr Y whom the doctors used to dread since once Mr Y starts he will not stop even after being asked to stop talking by the doctor. In those days the medical representatives used to talk about the products to the doctors using visual aids which used to be changed every month. Products being the same if one benefit is highlighted in one month the other benefit would be highlighted in the visual aid of the next month.

This medical representative went to the doctor and took out the visual aid and the doctor who knew this habitual talker immediately interrupted by saying that he has already seen the visual aid in order to avoid Mr Y. To the doctor's astonishment Mr Y immediately took out another visual aid and said, "Doctor this is last month's visual aid which you not have seen." And the doctor had no escape but to pretend hearing the boring talk.

His immediate supervisor used to be a fun loving guy and used to tell his colleagues that when Mr. Y starts talking to the doctor the supervisor used to sit on a stool near the door so as to escape no sooner the doctor starts yelling at Mr. Y.

This medical representative would not stop talking in spite the doctor bluntly telling "I am not listening to you Mr Y," or at times "I have turned a deaf ear towards you."

One needs to be very careful about what is being communicated, to whom it is being communicated, how it is being communicated and under what circumstances it is being communicated. How can we talk to a customer at length when he is required to rush somewhere urgently? The best way is to ask the customer what time will suit him so that we may approach the customer again?

Communication Gap

In a soft drink company the sales meet was being conducted by the training manager who was trying to impart selling skills to the salesmen who are usually semi-literate (high school or in some cases graduates) but have to work very hard in the market to sell the products of the company.

There was a salesman who had recently joined the company and earlier had worked in a mobile handset company for a very short time. The training manager asks this sales man how he would increase the volume of the business in his market and was amused to get the answer, "Sir, by pressing the button" and gesturing as if he is holding a mobile hand set and trying to increase the volume by pressing the volume button.

In the soft drinks industry it is very common to have daily market schemes which are usually announced when the trucks loaded with all the soft drinks variants leave the depot. In order that the competitor does not come to know of the scheme of the day it is whispered in the ears of the salesman by an executive who stands at the gate of the depot.

After the trucks leave the depot the executives also leave for their market work and catch up with a truck or two during the course of the day and help the salesmen in selling in the market.

At times the market scheme is a repeat of the last day's scheme. One day this was the case and the executive (let's call him Mr X) whispered this to all fifty salesmen.

After a while the sales head at the depot got a call and was surprised to hear Mr X on the other end asking what the scheme of the day was. When asked why he was asking about the scheme when he himself had informed all the salesmen about it, Mr X replied that he had merely told all the salesmen that it was a repeat of yesterday's scheme. When asked if he knew the scheme operated yesterday, Mr X replied with, "Sir, I was absent yesterday and that is why I am asking you!"

Learning: All business communication have a purpose and one needs to take utmost care while communicating and should know what is being communicated and should check whether the message has been received in the right perspective by the receiver or not.

In the above instance the executive should have first and foremost checked up from his fellow executives what was the scheme the day before. Then asked each and every sales man at the gate what was the yesterday's scheme to know whether all the salesmen knew the yesterday's scheme and then told them to implement the yesterday's scheme today too. There may have been salesmen who too were absent yesterday and may not know what the yesterday's scheme was!

Use the Brain, at least Occasionally

In a depot two litres pet bottles of soft drinks were about to get expired in 15 days. Once the expiry date is over the bottles cannot go to the market but have to be drained. Usually these kind of stocks are to be sold with heavy discounts in the market. Unfortunately this near expiry stocks of the two litres cola were meant for institution selling only and due to some technical hitch could not be given to the retail as well as wholesale market.

Instructions were received to sell the same on door to door basis. In this case the executives who are competent in canvassing as well as selling were to go with the truck and visit households and sell the same with an attractive scheme directly to the end user. Instructions were being implemented in letter and spirits. Executives with loaded vehicles 50c/s to 100c/s of soft drink two litres packs containing nine bottles each left the depot in their adventure of door to door selling.

It was also decided among the team members that the primary target would be housing societies as each society has approximately 100 to 200 flats. Some of the executives who could not enter some societies due to the rigid rules of not allowing outsiders, met the residents at the entrances nevertheless sold 40c/s to 70c/s on the first day.

Mr. X also went for door to door selling with gusto. In the evening it was discovered to the bewilderment of the sales head that an exhausted Mr. X had returned to the depot without selling even a single bottle, what to talk of a case of soft drink. On being questioned by the Sales Head Mr X replied, "Sir, I went to four societies but was denied entry since the rules of the societies were very rigid regarding outsider's entry".

The sales head asked why he hadn't gone to the kothies and bungalows at least. "Sir, but you never told to me to go to the bungalows or the kothis," replied Mr. X to the sales head who in order not to exhibit his anger had to immediately gulp a glass of cold water to calm his nerves which had started burning by then.

You Go First

Medical representatives in the good old days used to travel by buses to the nearby towns which were part of their assigned territories. Laden with their bags carrying medicines samples as well product literature they used to board these buses.

In those days hawkers selling pens, digestion pills and homemade tooth powders also used to get into the buses and sell their product to the passengers by canvassing for the same and get down the bus before the bus starts.

The hawkers also used to carry their product in bags or homemade jholas. Once a medical representative was to board a bus to a nearby town and a hawker who was also to get on the bus to sell and mistook the medical representative for a fellow hawker, told him courteously, “Go ahead, you may sell first in the bus.”

Chapter Nineteen

No My Way or Your Way, Only Our Way

One needs to act our way which is a refined form of my way and your way. If you stick to your way and I stick to my way then the things and the relationship shall go astray. In any business, relationship and teamwork we need to have **our way**. There needs to be a compromise so that the best of the ways are selected for implementation.

Even in marriage the husband and wife need to respect each other's views and at the same time make many compromises so the relationship strengthens and they live a happy married life. When the husband goes his way and the wife goes her way and each is adamant to follow their own way then there is unpleasantness in life. They may not go for divorce but shall not have the bond of love, trust and emotions without which married life will be mechanical.

Success cannot be without U.

A husband used to intimidate his wife. Every day he used to yell at her and say, "Get me warm water for bathing, or else!" The scared wife would immediately rush to the kitchen heat the water on the stove and bring it. This continued for a few days and the wife kept on obeying the husband. One day she mustered enough courage and when the husband shouted in his usual manner she retorted with, "Or else what?"

"Or else, I shall bathe with cold water," replied the husband.

It was merely a joke but there is learning in this joke too. The husband wanted to go **his way** and for a while the wife yielded to his wish. Ultimately one day she decided to go **her way** and rebuked her husband. But then that too wasn't quite right. There are times when hot water is essential for a bath. If the husband went **her way** then he might catch pneumonia.

So, the right way is **our way**—install a geyser! This way the husband is assured his hot water bath and the wife is saved the drudgery.

An idiotic conclusion but may well be right! Learning is a never ending process for we can learn from small incidences, books, internet, televisions, films and even jokes like the above illustration provided by the idiot.

The fact remains that the learning needs to be put in to practice every now and then so that it gets deeply embedded in the personality of the individual and becomes a habit and reflects in all the actions thoughts and eventually in the character itself. An individual who has learnt **to give** in the long run may become a philanthropist when the learning has been practiced regularly. I know of persons who donate 10% of their earnings for the benefit of the not so privileged or give it to the NGOs who are pursuing noble causes.

Chapter Twenty

How to Succeed in Making Cold Calls

It is seen nowadays that not even a single day passes when we do not receive a cold call from a bank for a loan, credit card companies or some online buying offer. Most of us get irritated by these frequent interruptions when one is engaged in some important activity.

It is observed that usually these cold callers are snubbed by the recipients of the cold calls. These calls usually do not yield any tangible results and we keep reading in the newspapers that these cold calls should be banned altogether.

How dare we make a sale without any investment in the customer? We have got to make some investment and give importance to the prospect in order to convert the prospect into our customer.

How can we make a sale in today's highly volatile marketing scenario just by making a telephone call? We have got to impress our customer and for this we have got to meet the customer in person. We have to impress our customer first and then make a sale.

Instead of calling the customer over telephone it is better that these aggressive companies should obtain the addresses of the prospective buyers and then send a small gift, may be a memento to the prospective customer and request them to call the company representative over telephone.

Initially only 2% may respond. Then the company needs to send one more letter after a fortnight with yet another gift informing the prospective customer that the company's representative shall call the customer at a specific time on a specific day. Now the customer maybe mentally prepared to take the company's representative call.

After two weeks send one more letter and one more gift and again request the customer to call or respond to the call and 50% will, since we have given them due importance by writing three letters and have given them respect by sending three gifts.

Out of 100 prospects even if we are able to make a sale to only 25% i.e. only 25 customers it is certainly worth a trial. We have sent three letters and three gifts say at the total cost of Rs 500 per prospective customer. The total amount invested in 100 customers is Rs 50,000/-. In case we are able to make a sale to 25 customers the cost per customer works out to Rs 2000/- each.

If we sincerely try, it may work but only if we have a conviction and try it with excellence (well drafted letter and thoughtful gifts).

Chapter Twenty One

First Impression Is the Last Impression

Impress but do not press for sale in the first meeting. There is always a second time.

It is an oft repeated adage that the first impression is the last impression and is everlasting since when we meet someone we may instantly develop a like or dislike for the person in the first meeting itself and thereafter the mind becomes preconditioned and starts harbouring preconceived notions which require a long time to change.

Have we ever thought of meeting our fiancée, girl friend, interviewer or even our boss, peers and the subordinates for the first time? We have all seen women, girls, men, children attending the marriage parties in the best of their dresses in order to leave a good first impression.

The same is true about customers also and it is all the more important to present ourselves well in front of the customers.

Here are a few business etiquette pointers which we may all know but not always practice:

- Are we in time to call upon the customer in case an appointment has been taken? We should not be late even by a minute and must show up on the dot. This knowledge is available to all of us but only having knowledge is not enough, it is the application which is more important. Believe it if we show up on the dot for the meeting 50% impression has already been made.

- We should be well dressed and smart in appearance. If we have driven a vehicle covering a long distance then we should try to have a wash before the meet.
- We should send our business card to the customer through the peon and wait outside till the time we are called to enter the customer's chamber. There are instances when the customer may take even an hour to call us. We should not panic since the time wasted in waiting is time invested. We can always do some reading while waiting. We can endeavour to know the customer better by having a chat with the receptionist, the peon or the other staff.
- In case we are called late we should always have the courtesy to tell the customer that we are well aware of how hard-pressed the customer is for time and must thank him profusely for the time he has spared out of his busy schedule.
- We must look enthusiastic and cheerful and greet the prospect/customer with a genuine smile.
- We must enter the room of the customer after taking permission.
- We should not take a seat until asked to by the customer. By keeping standing we are in fact giving the importance and respect to the customer.
- We should not start the talk till the time customer asks us to talk. There are instances when the sales guys start their talk when the customer is busy over the telephone or is working on the computer.
- We should be enthusiastic in our talk and you should be able to make the customer enthusiastic in taking a positive decision in our favour.
- We should be able to maintain an eye contact with the customer.
- We may not be successful in the first meeting nevertheless we should try to extract a commitment as to when the

customer would like to meet us again.

- We should try to follow up the first meeting with a letter or e-mail of thanks.
- We should try to send a small memento to the customer as a follow up if not given in the first meeting.
- We should try to find out the likes and dislikes of the customer and plan strategy accordingly.
- We should go all out to IMPRESS the customer but avoid pressing the prospect or customer harder for order during the first meeting itself.
- Have we rehearsed as to what we will talk about, the company we represent and the product we are going to talk about? If Mr. Amitabh Bachchan can come to the sets on the dot then why can't we? We are the hero of the shoot of the movie THE IMPRESSION about to be shot with the customer in the second lead role and the shot needs to be okayed in the first take itself.
- Time is very precious and the customer's is all the more precious. We should try to be brief when making a presentation or talking to the customer. If we are convinced that the customer is really taking great interest in our talk then we may go on and on with the customer's permission.
- We should not just see but observe the customer as well as the situation. Observing provides us an opportunity to analyze the personality as well as the situation.
- The customer who is not interested in the discussion may start looking at the watch or may call the peon and give some instructions or may start doing some work on the computer providing us a hint that we should leave else the customer shall show us the door.
- This hint should be sufficient and we should profusely thank the customer for having spared the valuable time and also thank for granting an opportunity to meet.

- Every time we meet a customer we should not try to show too much of familiarity since we do not know the circumstances under which we are meeting them.
- A customer who is not in a good mood may turn down the best of offers. We should therefore ascertain the mood, the circumstances and analyze the situation and then act accordingly.
- There is always a second time to make a sale and we should have patience and keep on trying to be victorious one day.
- We should try to talk to the customer in a language well understood by the customer and also we should try and make sense of what makes the customer tick. Once we are able to identify this we can plan and act accordingly.
- A customer having a passion for cricket should be talked to about cricket instead of hockey which the customer may not like. Similarly a customer fond of films should not be talked to about cricket. Knowing the customer is very important for success in sales.
- We should always try to keep the chair used for the interview in its original position in case we have changed the position while sitting.
- We should not bang the door while leaving the customer's chamber, instead the door should be shut softly and never should we leave the door open.

Chapter Twenty Two

The Right Way to Present Your Visiting Card

Your visiting card is one of your marketing tools and it plays a vital role when it comes to your introduction to a customer. Hence, it is important to present it in an impressive way. When a customer asks us for our visiting card, if we start searching for it in the pocket of our coat, shirt and trouser, having not found one, then desperately start searching our bag and finally fishing out a crumpled visiting card to hand it over to the customer will, definitely make the customer form a poor opinion about us. We will not only appear as unprofessional but also given with a good reason to doubt about our credentials.

How to let your Visiting Card Talk for you?

Hereunder are some professional ways to present your visiting card:

Your Visiting Card is **You**

We need to be very careful about the visiting card as it reads far more than the words written on it. Take a moment to have a close look at your visiting card, then try and find how we are seen through it.

A Crisp and Impressive Visiting Card

If your card is crumpled, it reflects a poor self-identity. A crisp visiting card taken out of an impressive card holder leaves a good impression. A good visiting card presented in a professional way to the prospective customer makes a very good first impression. So the need to invest in a very good quality visiting card is of paramount importance.

Do not Waste Time Searching for the Card

Searching for the visiting card leaves a very poor impression upon the prospect. You should be able to take out the visiting card and hand it over to the prospective customer in two seconds. The prospect's time is valuable and should not be wasted in search of the card.

Hand Over the Card while Standing, Giving respect to the Card as well as the Customer

While handing over the visiting card to the prospect, it is always better to stand up and hand over the card since this gesture tells that you accord respect to the visiting card as well as to the customer. Always hold the visiting card horizontally with both the hands with your name facing the customer.

Give a brief Introduction of Yourself and the kind of business you are Into...

While handing over the visiting card always give a brief description of yourself and your background for about ten seconds. The card should be presented with a view that the customer is able to read the material written on the card.

Always Stand Up while Receiving a Visiting Card from a customer and then Read the Customer's Name and Greet the Customer Aloud e.g. *"Good morning Mr. Z. It is my pleasure to meet you".*

Chapter Twenty Three

Pamper Your Boss to Become his Blue Eyed Boy

Observe the Following **Don'ts**

It is better not to argue with your boss. An argumentative subordinate is not liked by the boss. Hence arguments with peers and bosses should always be avoided.

In a meeting it is advisable that your cell phone is in a silent mode since you may be disturbing others in the meeting if your cell phone rings up frequently and which will certainly irritate your boss. While discussing with your boss it is always better to put your cell in the silent mode since your boss gets irritated when you take a call during the discussion. Boss also hates employees peeping on their cell phones while at work.

Proper communication between the bosses and the employees is the key to success of any organization. Good communication skills are appreciated by the boss whereas ineffective communication skills irritate the boss. If you are not able to complete an assignment within a given timeframe, it is advisable to give a valid reason to your boss instead of waiting for a reminder from a boss or give excuses.

You are sick and taking a sick leave, that's fine. You are not sick and taking leave and telling your boss that you are sick is, really an annoying thing that your boss hates.

Boss obviously develops a dislike to those employees who display poor table manners during a luncheon meeting with a client. Always observe good table manners when you are with a client during a luncheon as lousy table manners can cause embarrassment in front of the client and annoy your boss.

Employees who say one thing and do another are not liked by the boss. The employees who give flimsy excuses for not completing an assignment in time adds to the boss's irritation.

Employees who have a habit of arriving late to the office and leave early are not liked by the boss. Hence, be punctual to report for work and do not leave office early.

Always maintain a good hygiene when coming to office. Dress up properly and come to office since employees who are clumsy are not liked by the boss.

Do not discuss your personal problems with the boss. Boss does not like employees who discuss their personal problems in order to gain sympathy.

Chapter Twenty Four

Wisdom Thoughts

Thanks for reading the book AN IDIOT WHO SOLD A SHIP written by a common man who has practiced excellence and has been highly successful professionally and personally. By reading my book, you have encouraged me and I shall owe you a debt of sincere gratitude for this kind gesture. You will be pleased to know that this book is being appreciated by readers all over for its simple yet powerful contents illustrated in very interesting way through short stories, anecdotes and live examples. The readers have liked the simple yet practical approach towards successful selling and purposeful living. In case you are able to put to rigorous practice some learnings which have appealed to your heart and soul you will really stand to gain in professional and personal life.

It is primarily the actions which are more important than having the knowledge alone. Whatever in the book has appealed to your heart needs to be put to practice and then only you will be benefited in personal and professional life.

You are what your thoughts and action are. Kindly therefore set an objective patiently keeping in view of all the pros and cons and thereafter pursue it impatiently and whole heartedly and do not give up till the time you succeed to accomplish the desired results.

A team leader should know his team members as individuals and then deal with them accordingly and give the credit of success to the team and in case of failure have the guts to take the blame. A leader should try to earn the respect of the team.

Put in focused efforts of excellence to succeed in any project.

Customer is the king and he is obliging us by giving us an opportunity to serve him, hence we should leave no stone unturned to earn customer's satisfaction and make him our loyal customer. Always look for an opportunity to serve the customer and keep the business dealing transparent as far as possible.

See a dream and there after put in best efforts to realize the dream.

Try and fail instead of not trying at all.

HRD department should endeavour to select best of candidates during interviews and thereafter develop them for the job by imparting the desired skills which will make them competent and to have genuine will to retain the talented employees.

Organizations should endeavour to keep their employees satisfied so that they become more productive and are always motivated to meet any challenge.

When we have a choice in the morning to choose between happiness and unhappiness, why not to choose happiness which is a better choice and happiness is only a mindset. If we think we are happy we become happy.

Be a good human being and do good to other human beings and in turn good shall happen to you sooner or later.

Perform good *karmas* during your tenure on the planet earth so that you leave a mark in the hearts of other human beings for your good deeds.

By virtue of the above you shall lead a successful professional life and a purposeful personal life.

❑❑❑

New Arrivals

₹ 125/-

Tomorrow's Young achievers

31 career defining insights for a radically different tomorrow

Through this book the author wishes to share with Young Minds, lessons acquired through his academic sojourn at the prestigious Northwestern University (USA) and subsequent work activities, encompassing anecdotes, observations and learning drawn from personal experience, subject matter experts, ex-colleagues and specific classmates that culminates into 31 career defining insights to prepare young Minds for a radically different tomorrow.

Highlights:

- What happens when you are pleasantly coerced to experiment outside your 'comfort zone' by a creative genius?

Playing safe is one of the biggest risks in the 21st century. To prosper, you will have to take 'uncommon' risks even in a job.

It is possible for 'inexperienced' young minds to create entrepreneurial history.

Tomorrow's CEOs will come from the HR and PR domain.

Taming The Little Devils Within

; Never Too Late To Be What You Might Have Been

₹ 175/-

aving psychological problems are a part of everyone's life id a matter of degree. Knowing the degree is important ecause it is that which will decide your mental health status id the course of action to be followed. You will also realize iat most of the problems are self-created and our rigid titudes prevent us from making adjustments and changing ır lifestyles or ourselves. The advice given in this book is › be followed until it becomes a habit. It is to be followed ɔt only by people who suffer from a psychological problem ut also by all if they want to continue having a good mental ealth.

his book is written based on years of my practical experience and the approach to the problems ; dealt in a unique way. This book is unique because it will not only educate you about the arious common psychological problems but also enable you to measure/test yourself on iem. The measures will let you know if you suffer from one and, if so, to what degree.

---

www.unicornbooks.in • **email:** info@unicornbooks.in • www.pustakmahal.com

New Arrivals

freelance WRITING

for the 'Newbie' Writer

Freelance Writing for the 'Newbie' Writer attemp to demystify the whole concept of creative freelan writing even while bringing out its pitfalls. The boo highlights issues like importance of languag niche writing, querying an editor, reviewing a boo how to spot and avoid scams, plagiarism, and th requirements for publishing a book, etc.

It is essentially an introduction to the art of ho to make your writing 'work' for you, as a newb freelancer, needing to make a living out of it. Th book does not tell you how to write. Instead, it tells you what to expect and wh not to expect while you 'freelance' write.

HOW TO BECOME A SUCCESSFUL **ORATOR**

A complete guide to hone your presentation skills

Effective communication with the audience is an essential element to jumpstart your career. This practical and easy to use book will show you how to influence your audience with crisp and immaculate presentations. Its lively style and down-to-earth advice will help you to master all the skills required for those high impact presentations which would put you in the driver's seat in your profession. ***Features:*** Active listening skills, accent neutralisation, self management skills, composing the draft, using humour in the presentation, creating great visuals" both for OHP as well as for PowerPoint, memorising the presentation, conquering the presentation anxiety, presentation delivery, effective use of body language and handling the presentation emergencies.

A special feature of the book comprises more than 100 illustrations and cartoons that make the tips easy to grasp and easier to apply. Once you act on the advice given in this book, you will be amazed to see how effortlessly the "terrible" presentations and presenters are converted into the "terrific" ones.